This color charts book belongs to

_____

_____

Copyright © 2020. All rights reserved

No part of this publication may be reproduced, distributed or transmitted in any form or by any means

without written permission from the author or the publisher.

Introduction

This color charts book will help you to keep your art supplies organized and record all colors in one place.

It will allow you to easily find the ideal colors to complete your coloring or make comparisons to decide the right shade to use. You can also complete this color chart by type of color by simply specifying by reference the name of the felt pen or colored pencil.

120 separate color charts with hundreds of boxes will allow you to gather the ideal colors to organize and achieve the best coloring. You can thus adapt the use of this book to your needs and complete your color charts in a very artistic way.

Enjoy !

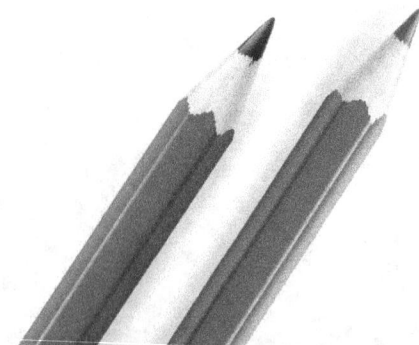
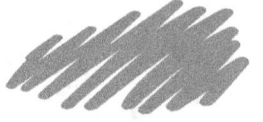

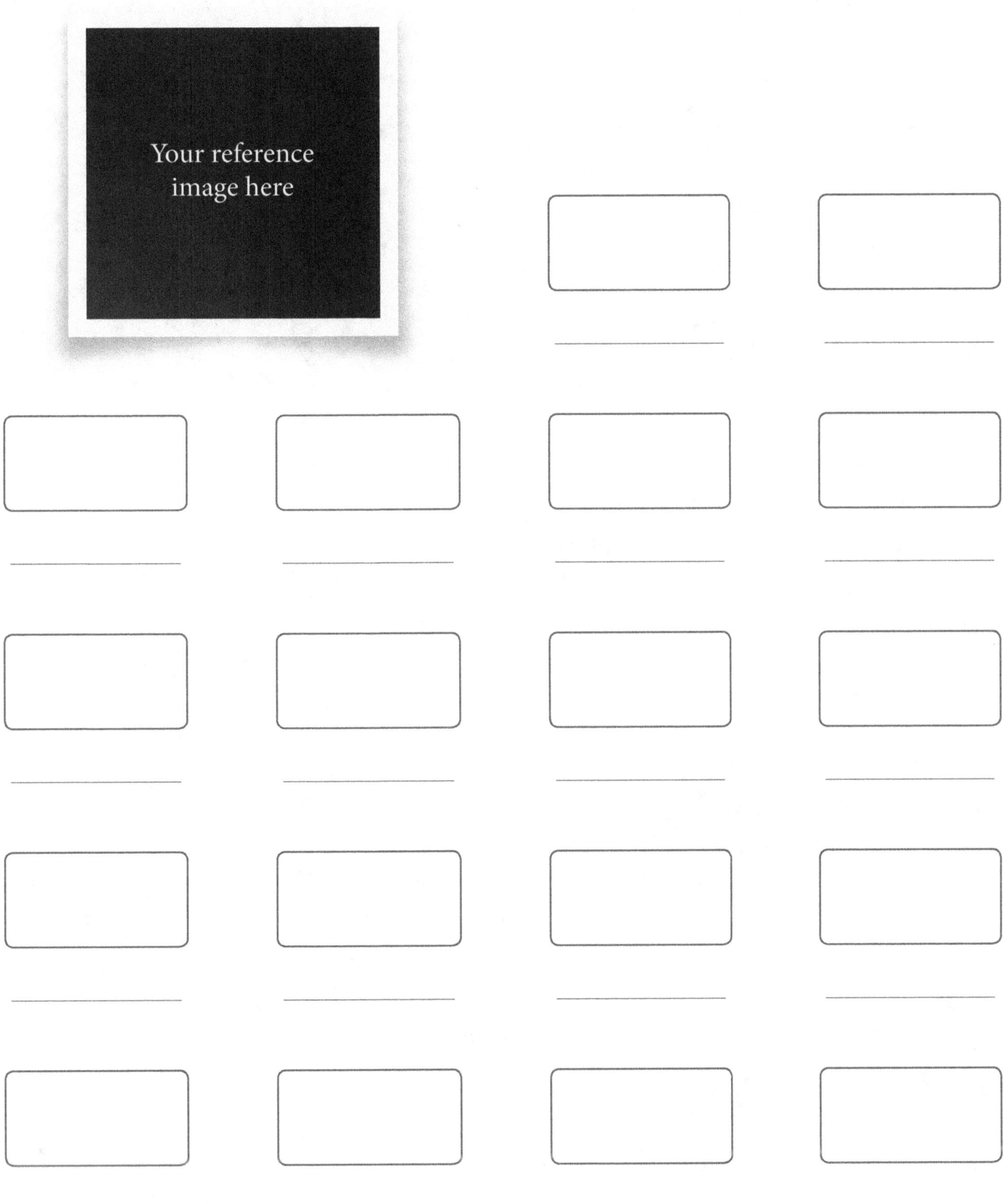

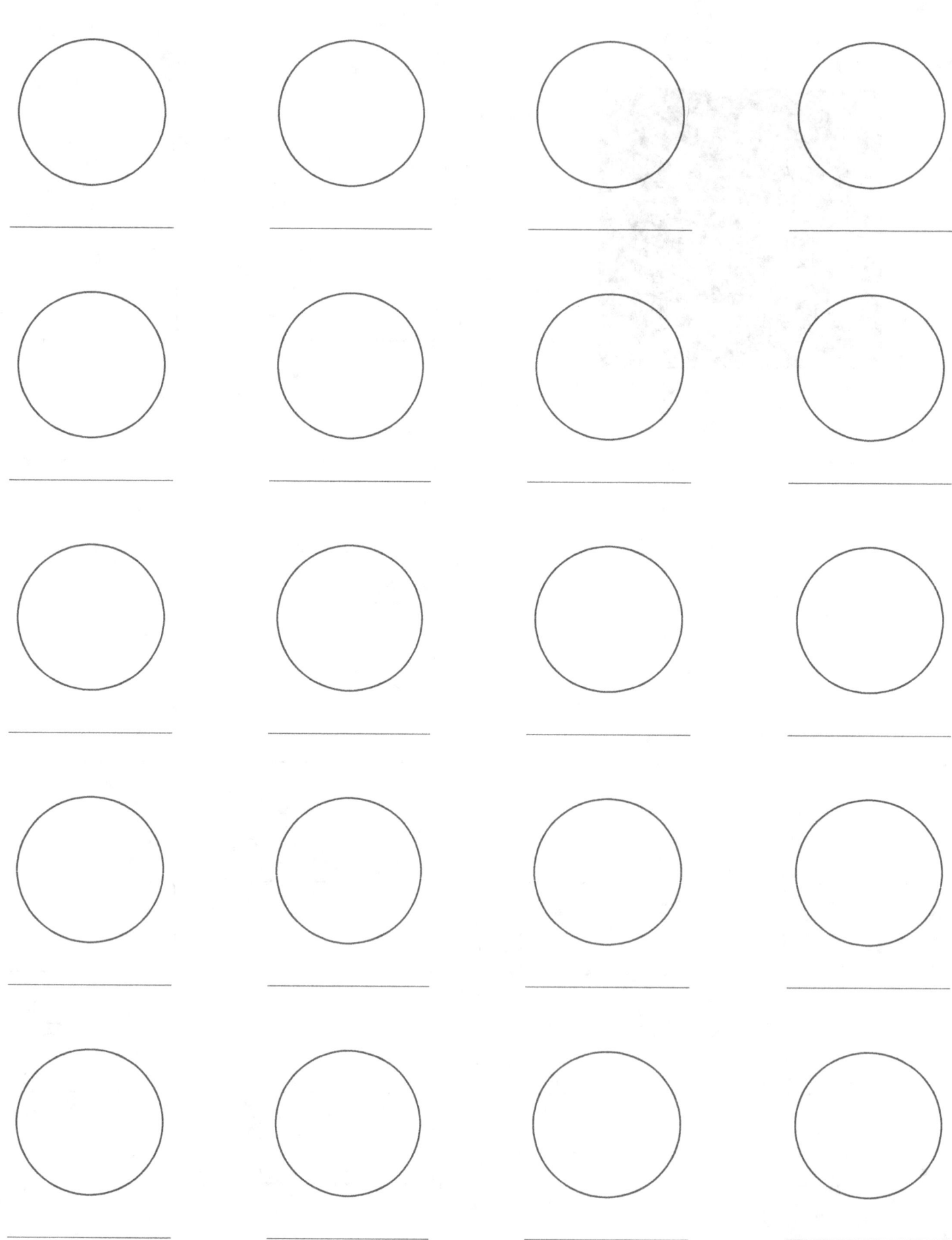

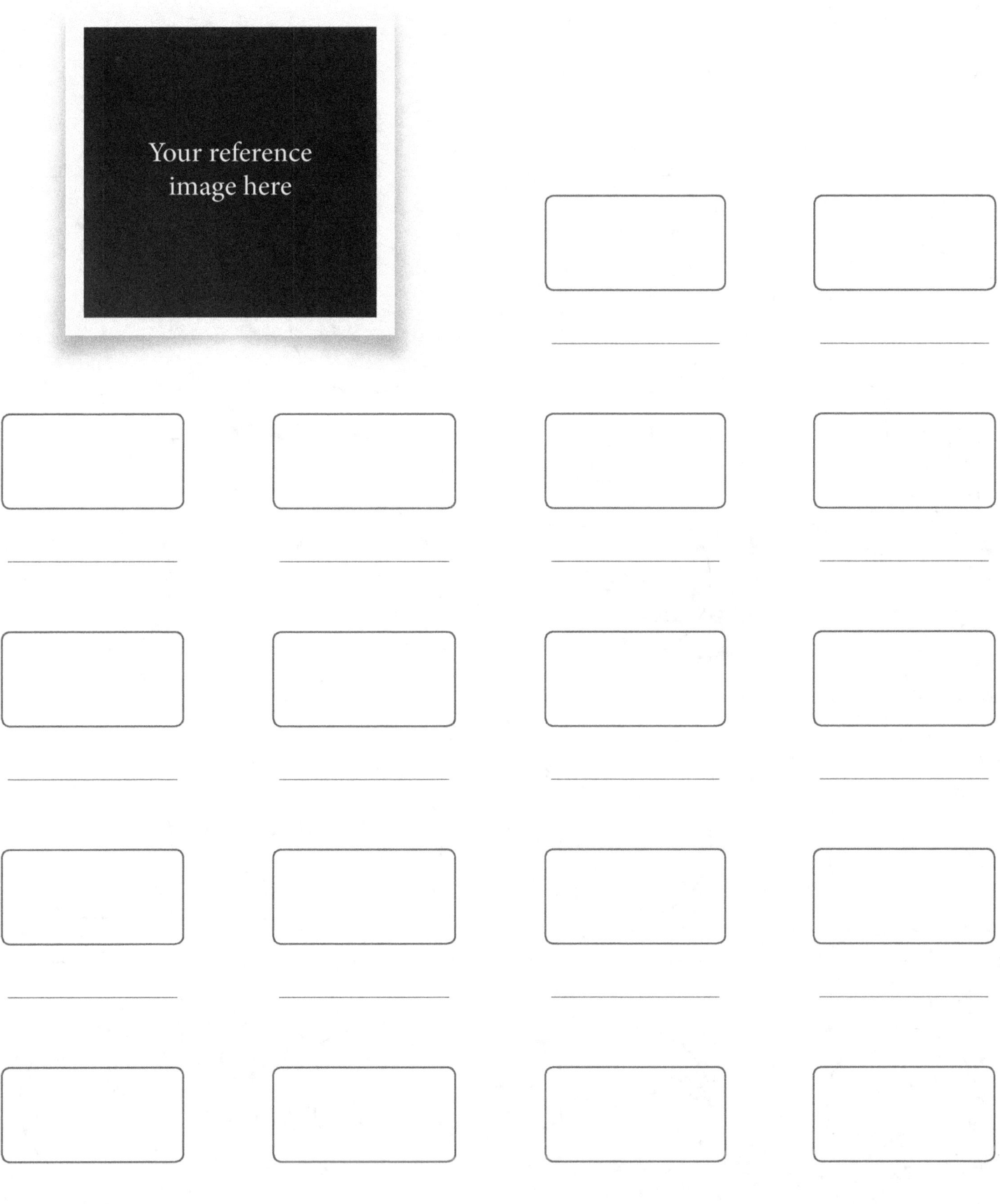

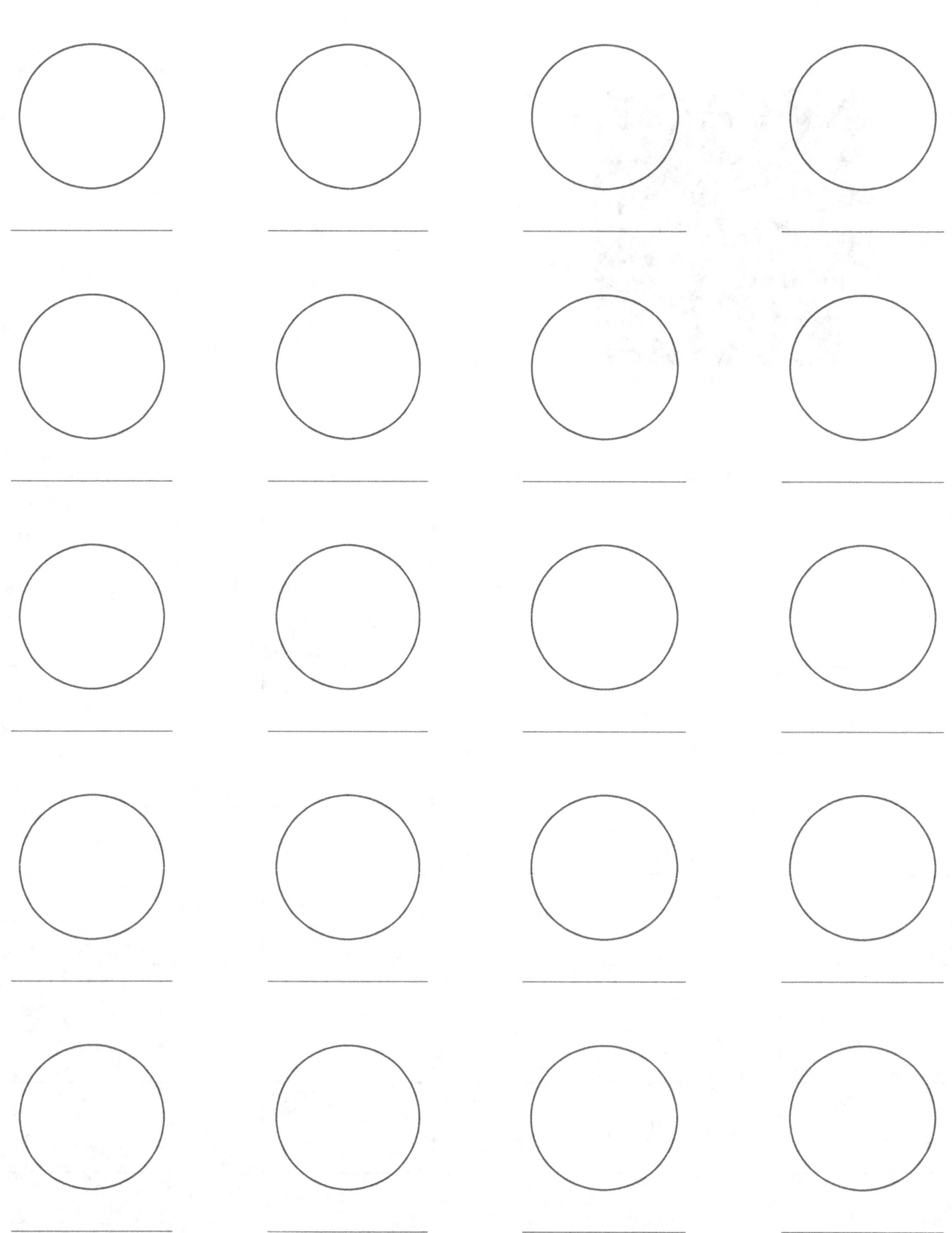

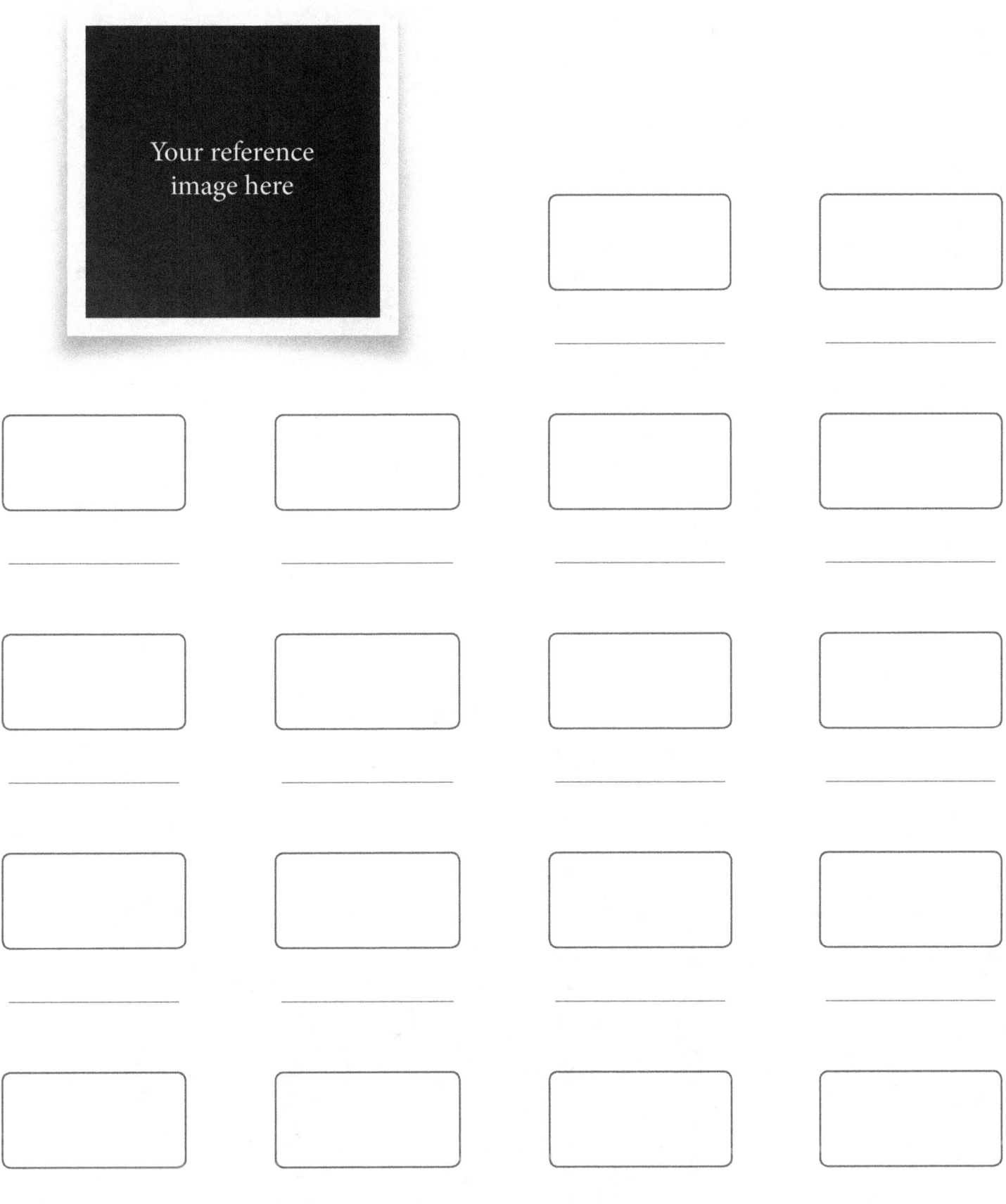

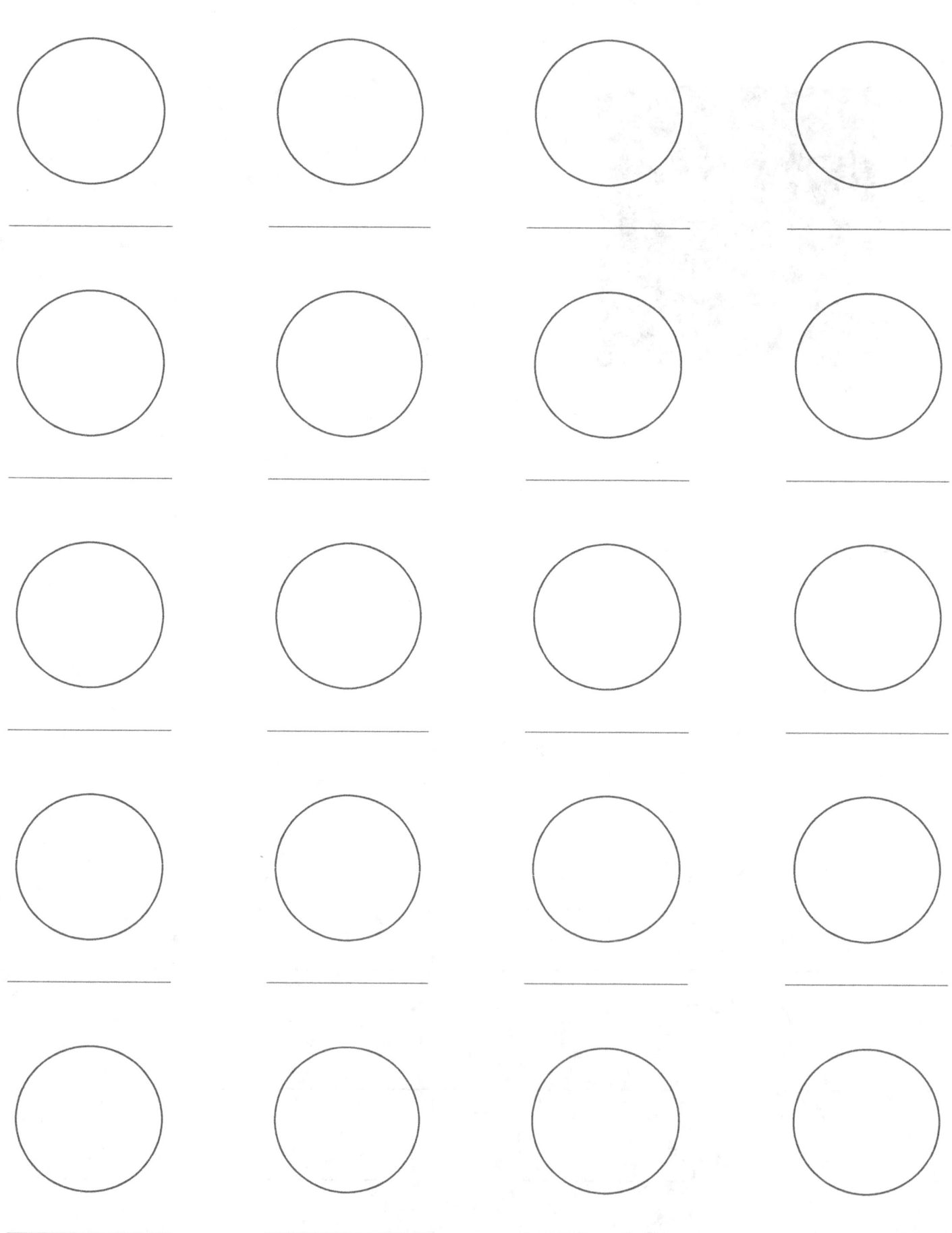

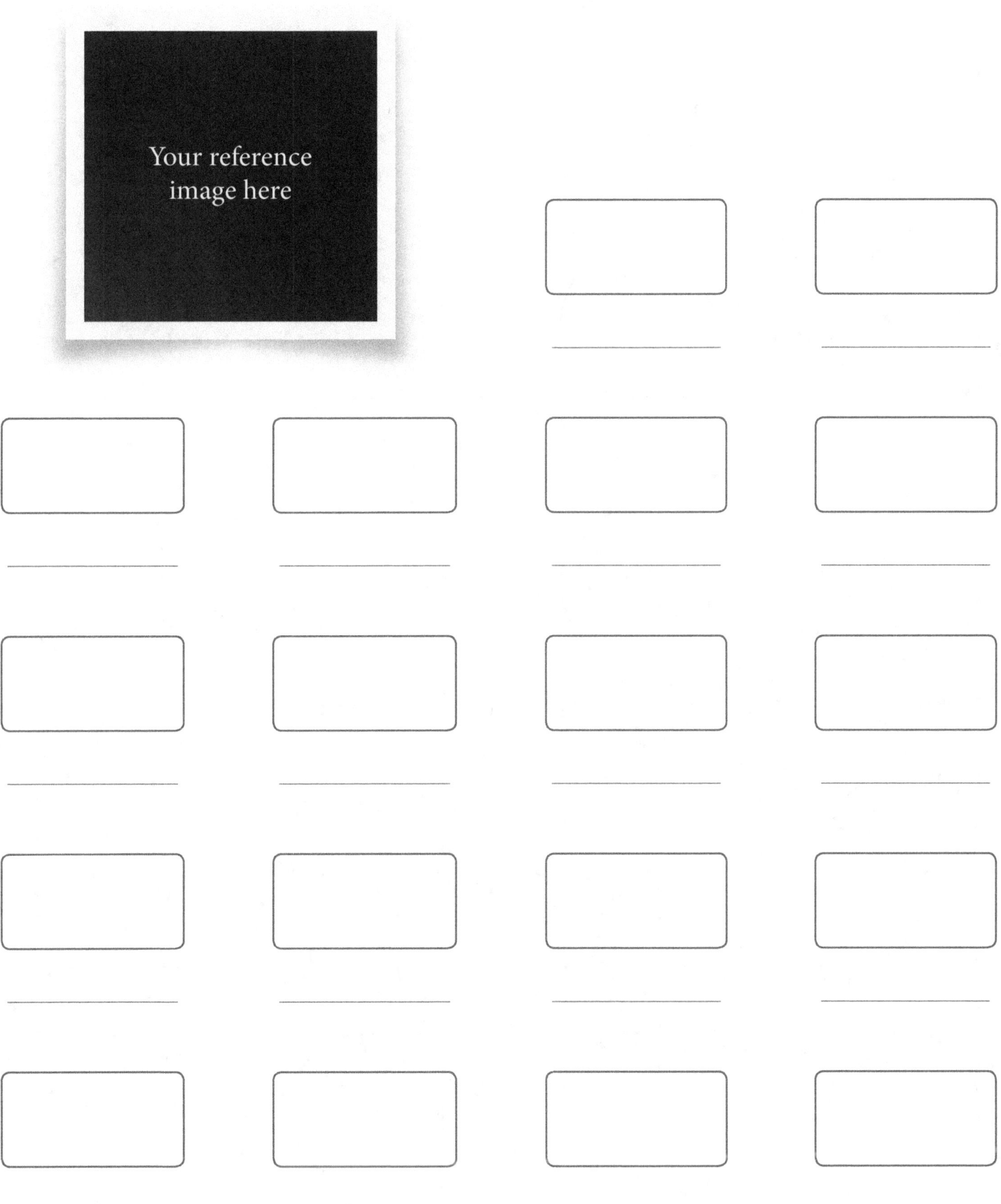

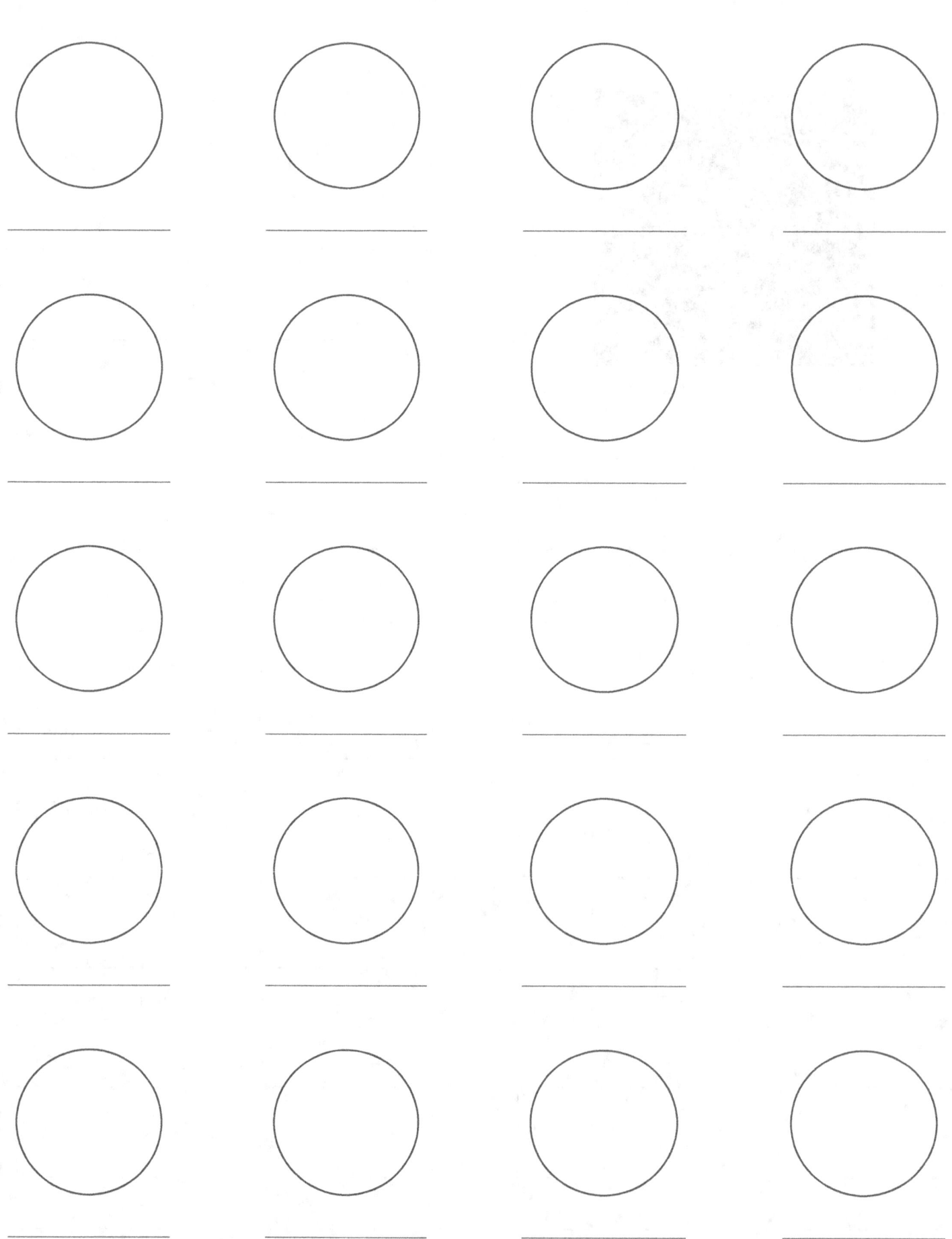

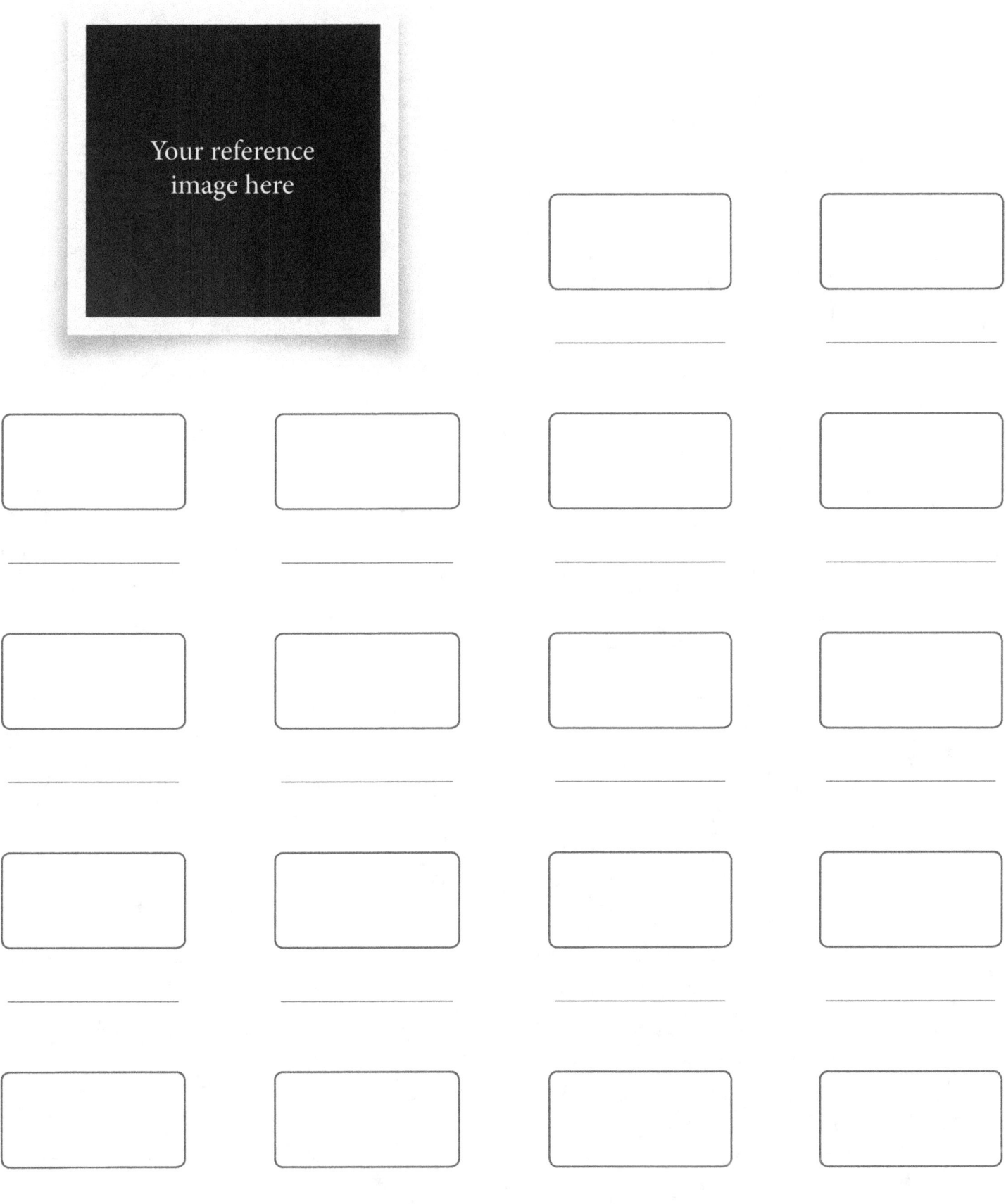

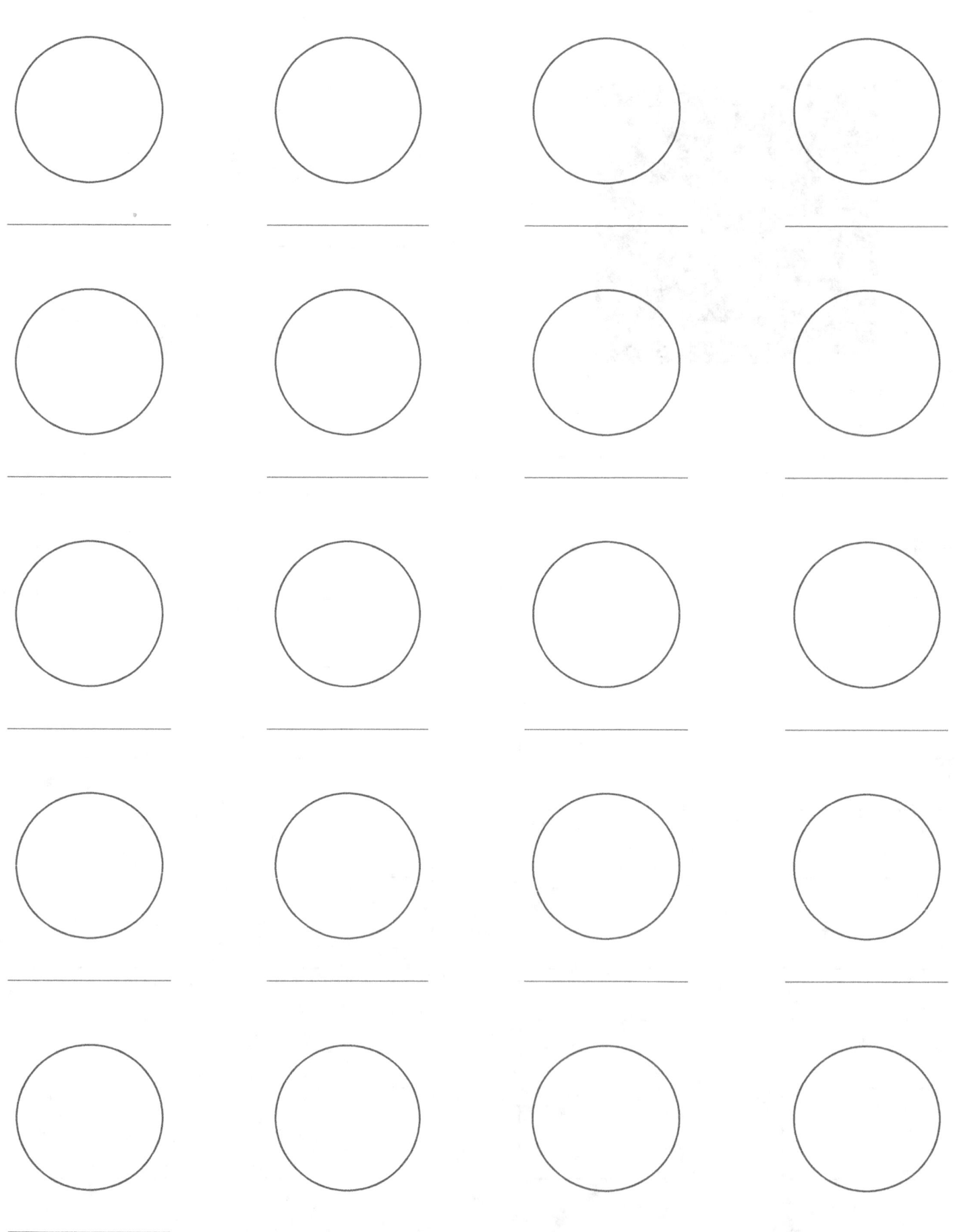

Your reference image here

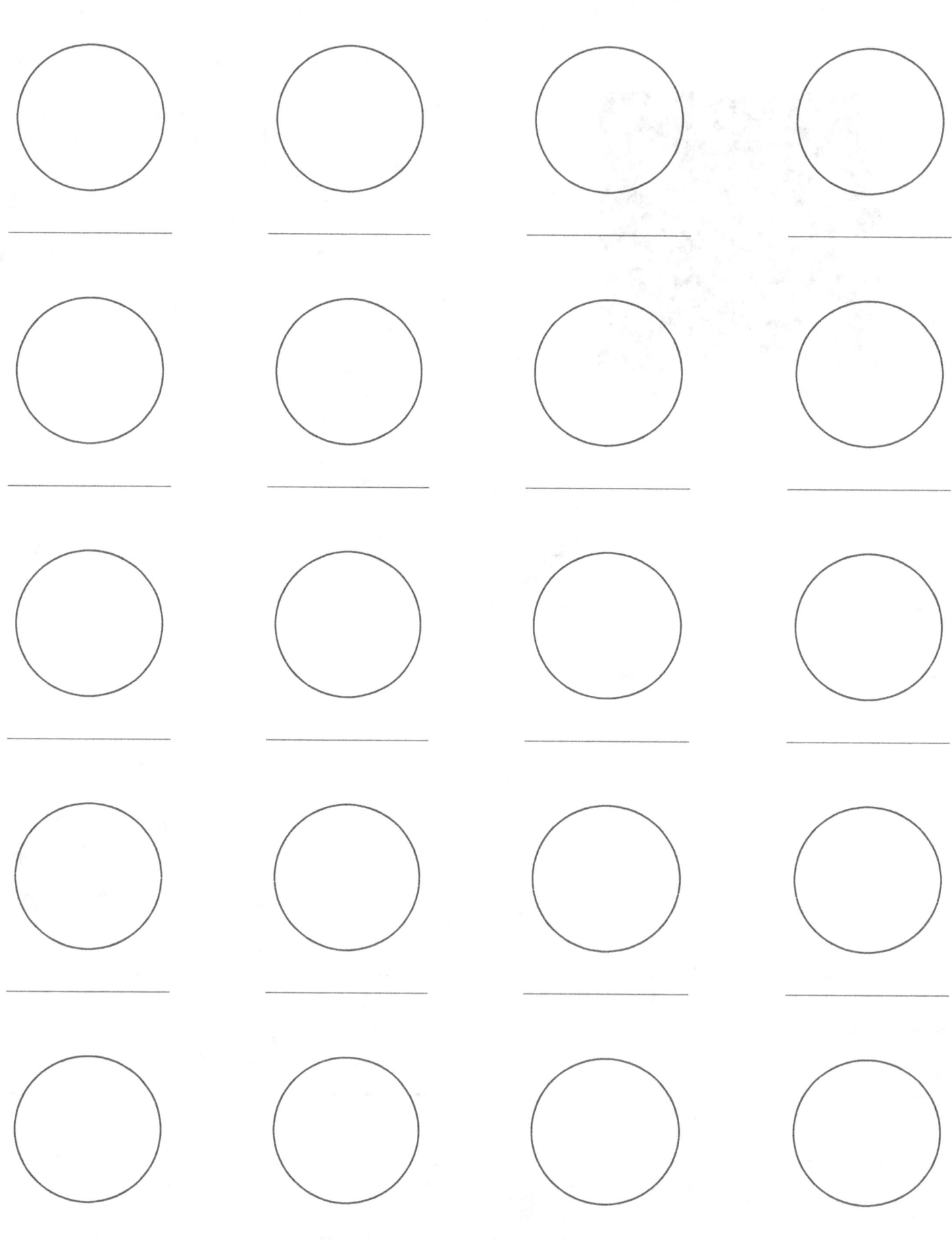

Your reference
image here

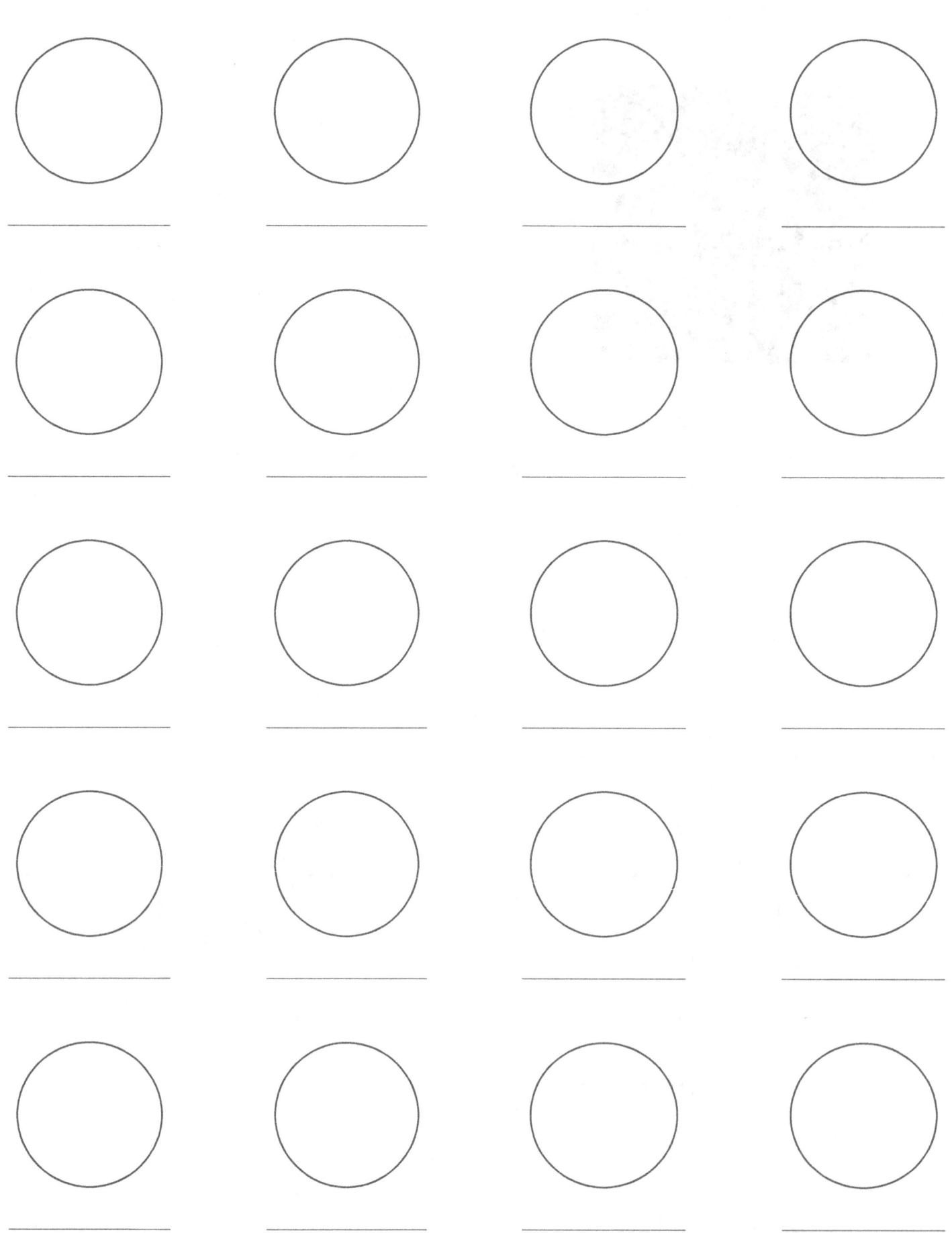

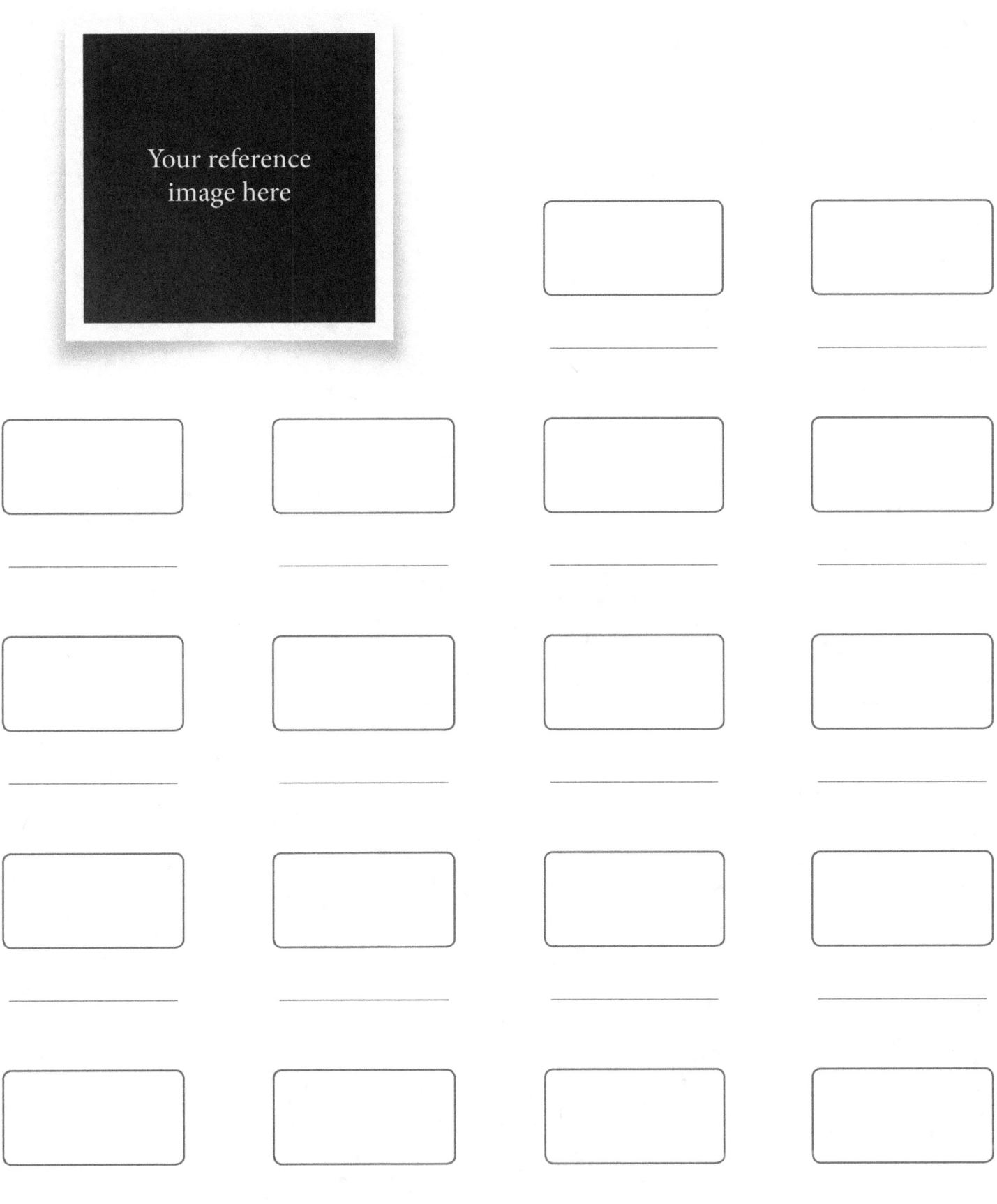

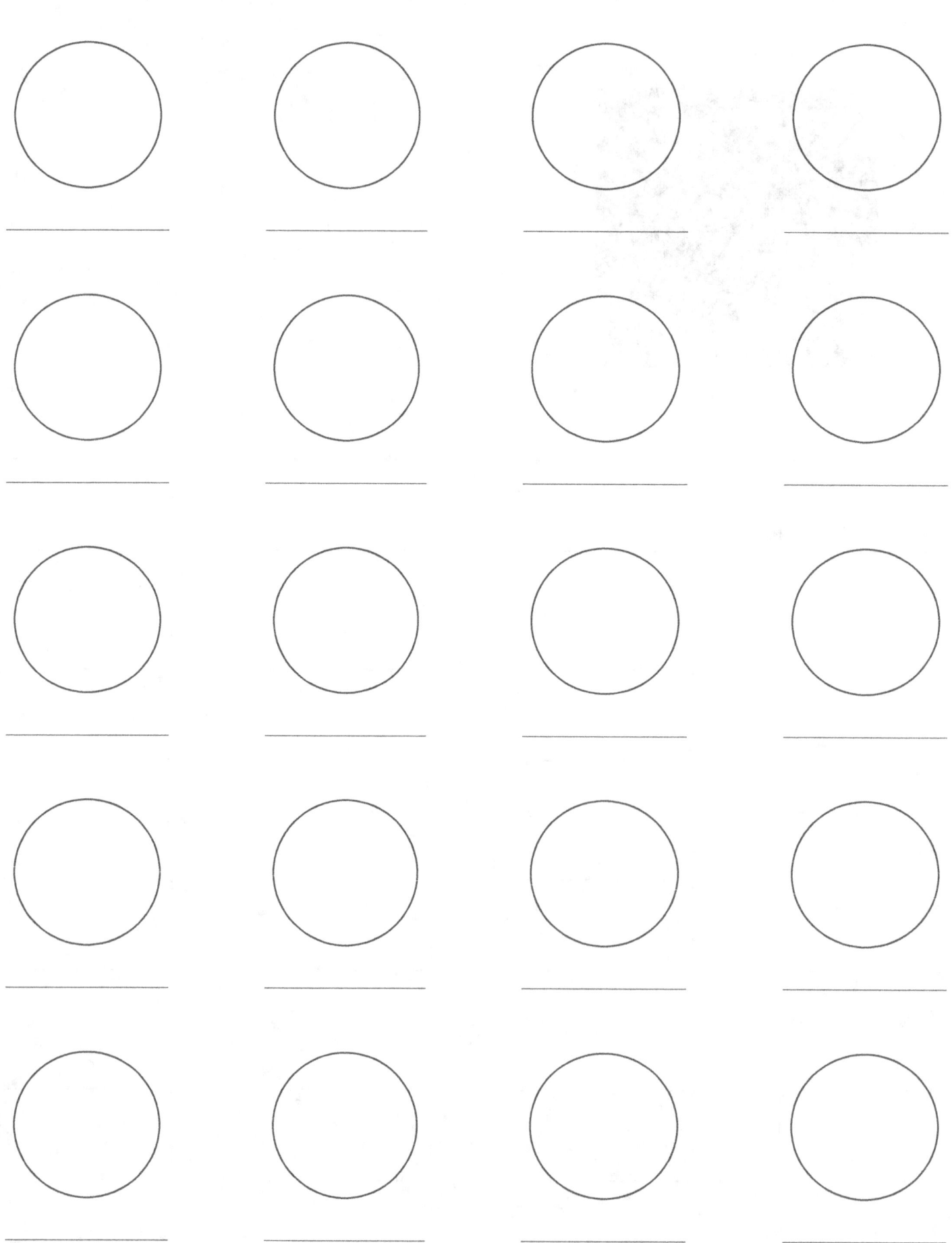

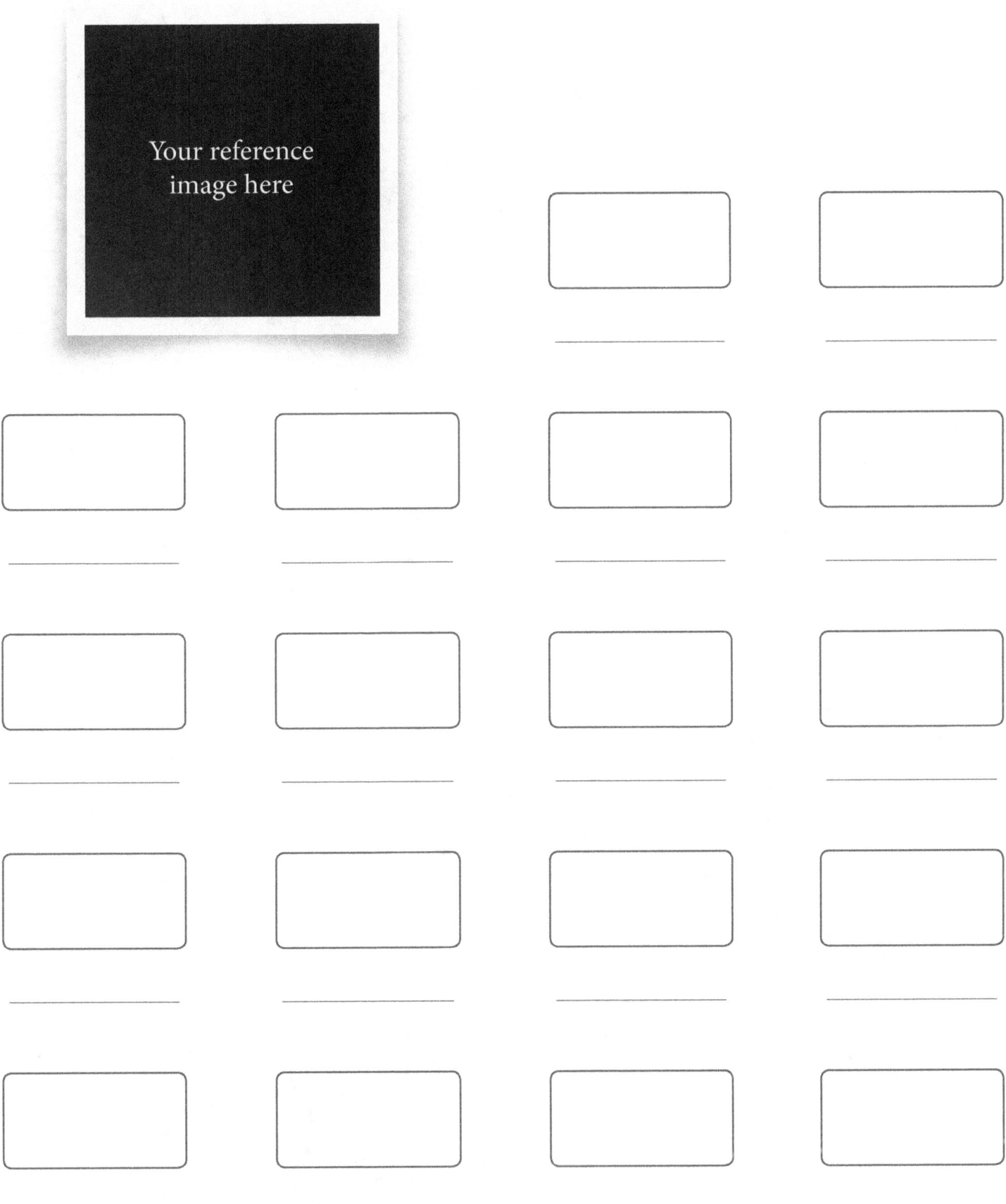

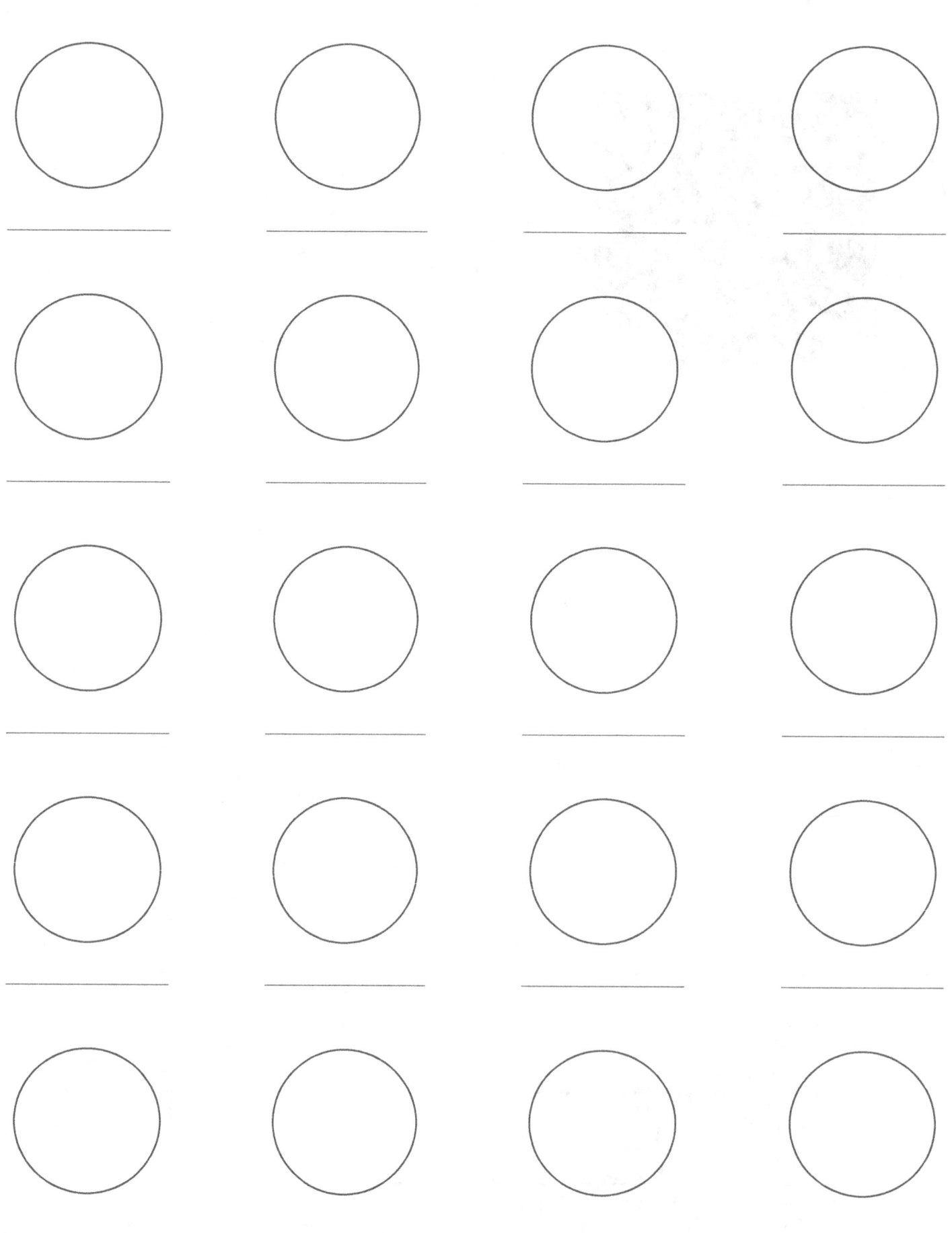

Your reference image here

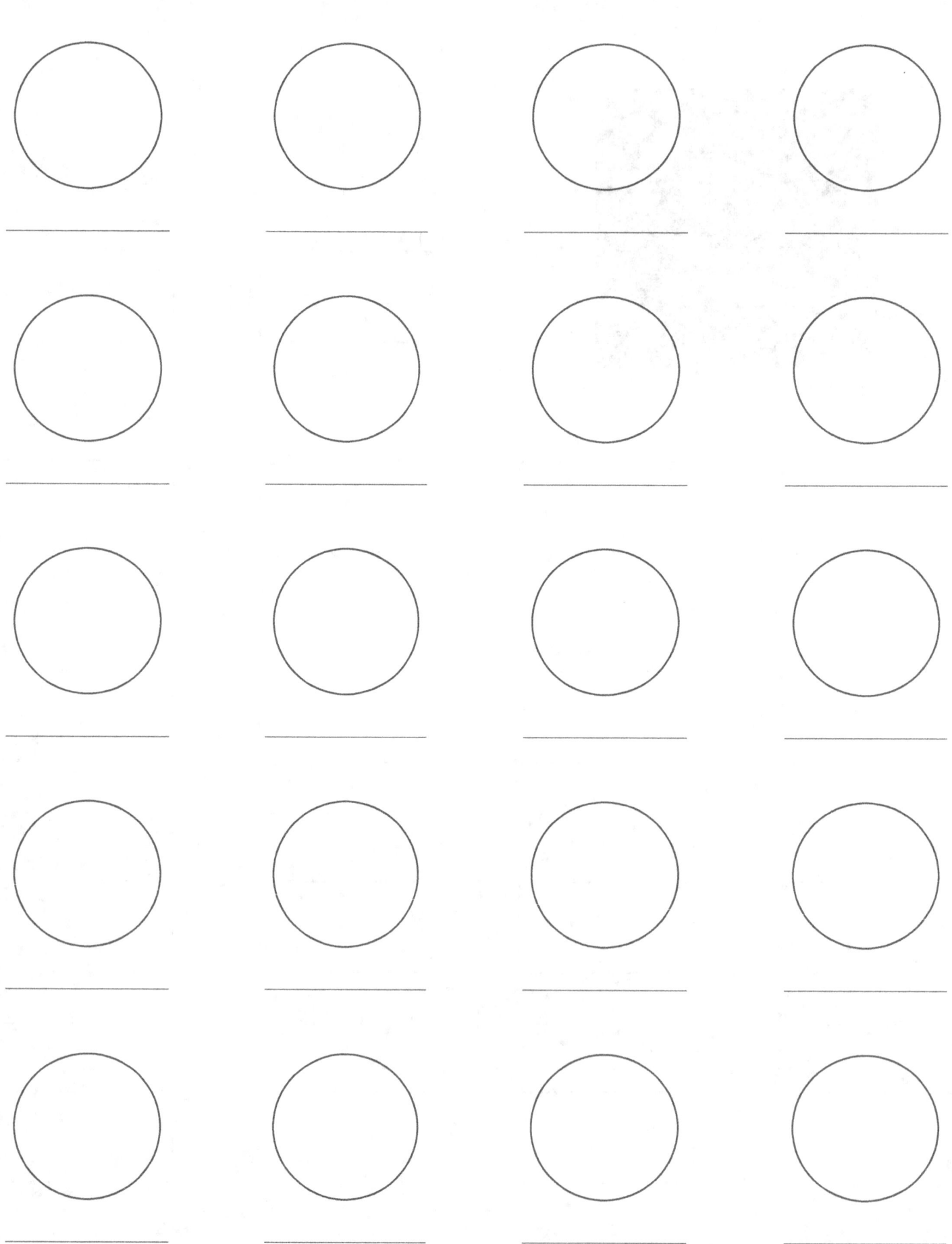

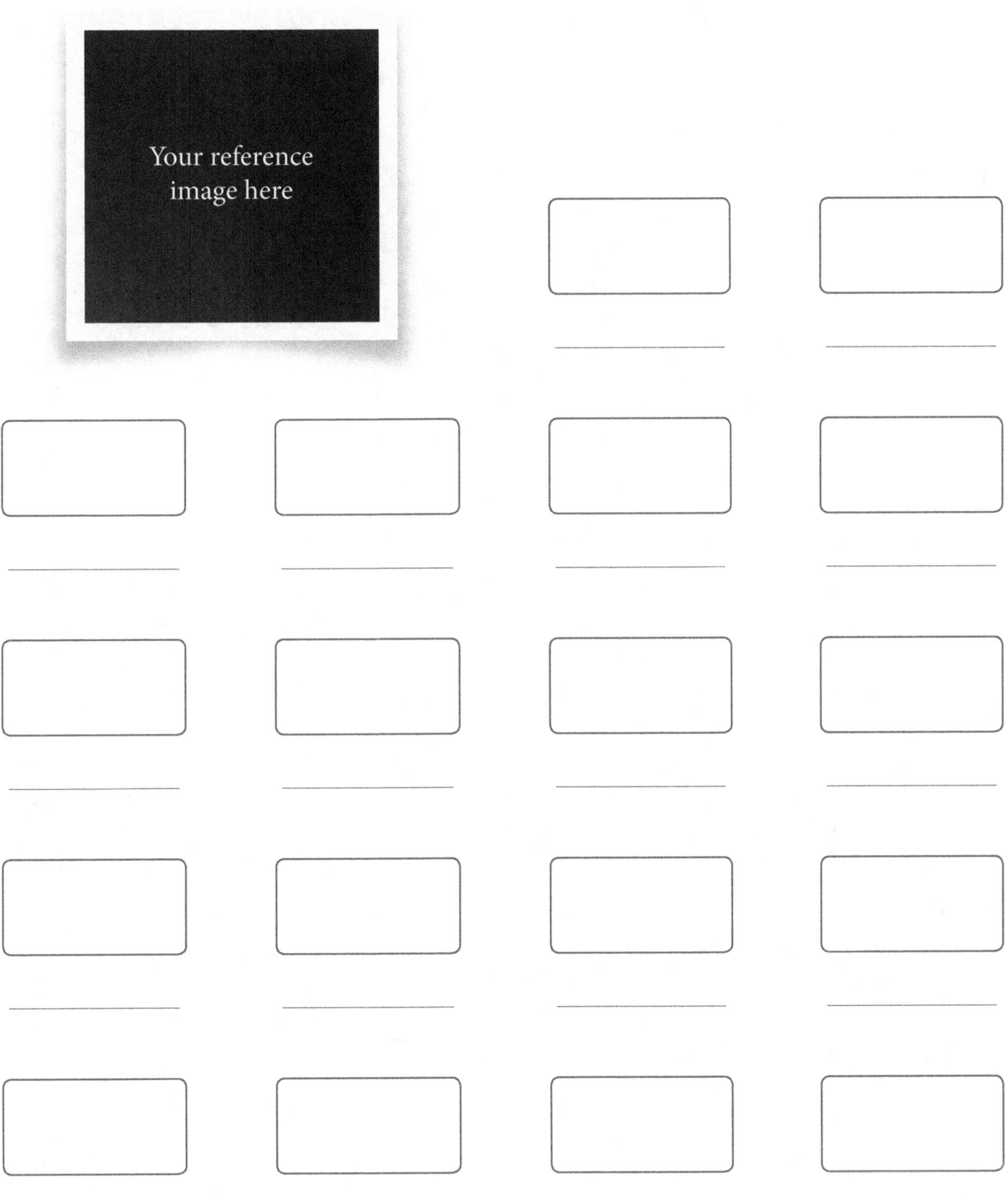

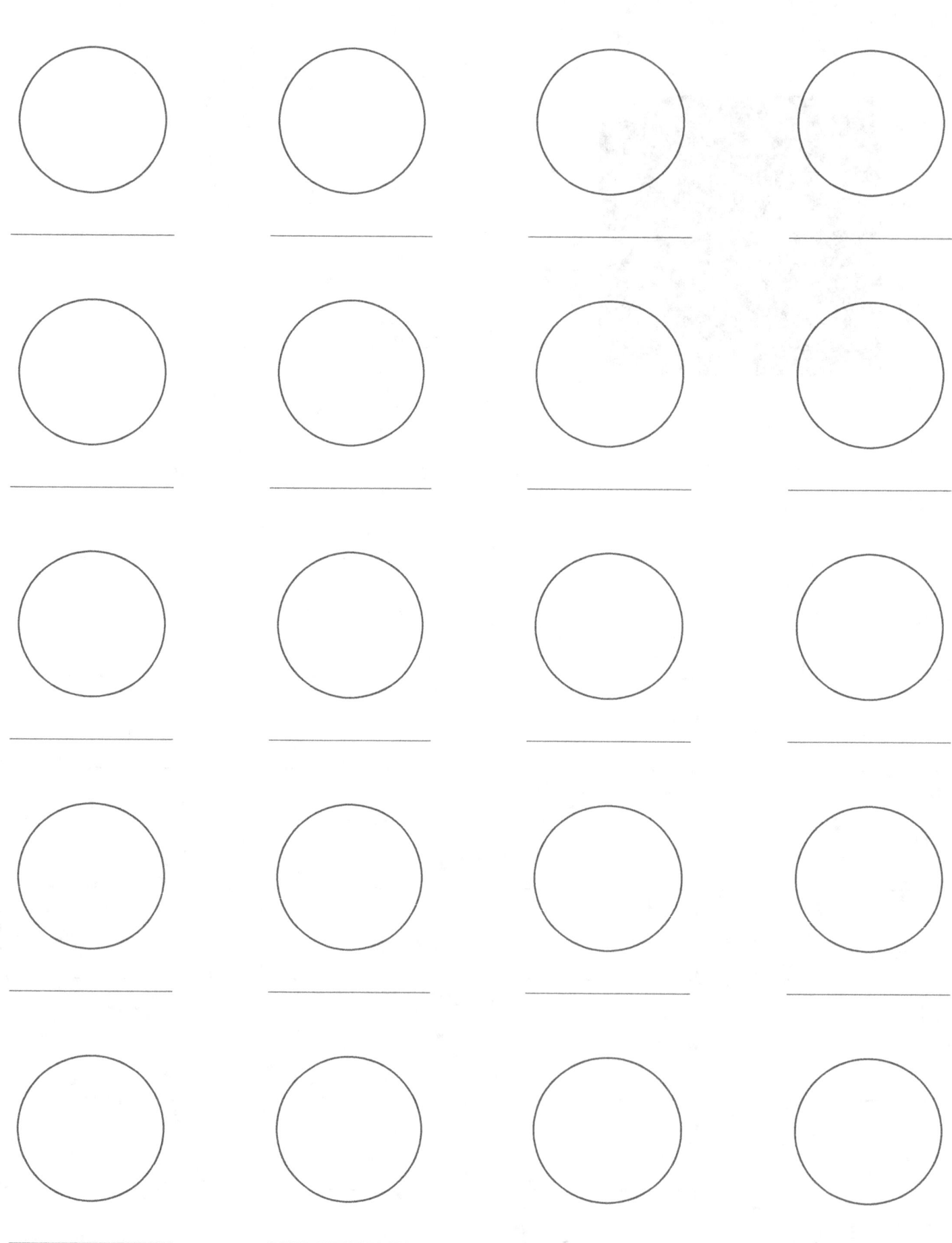

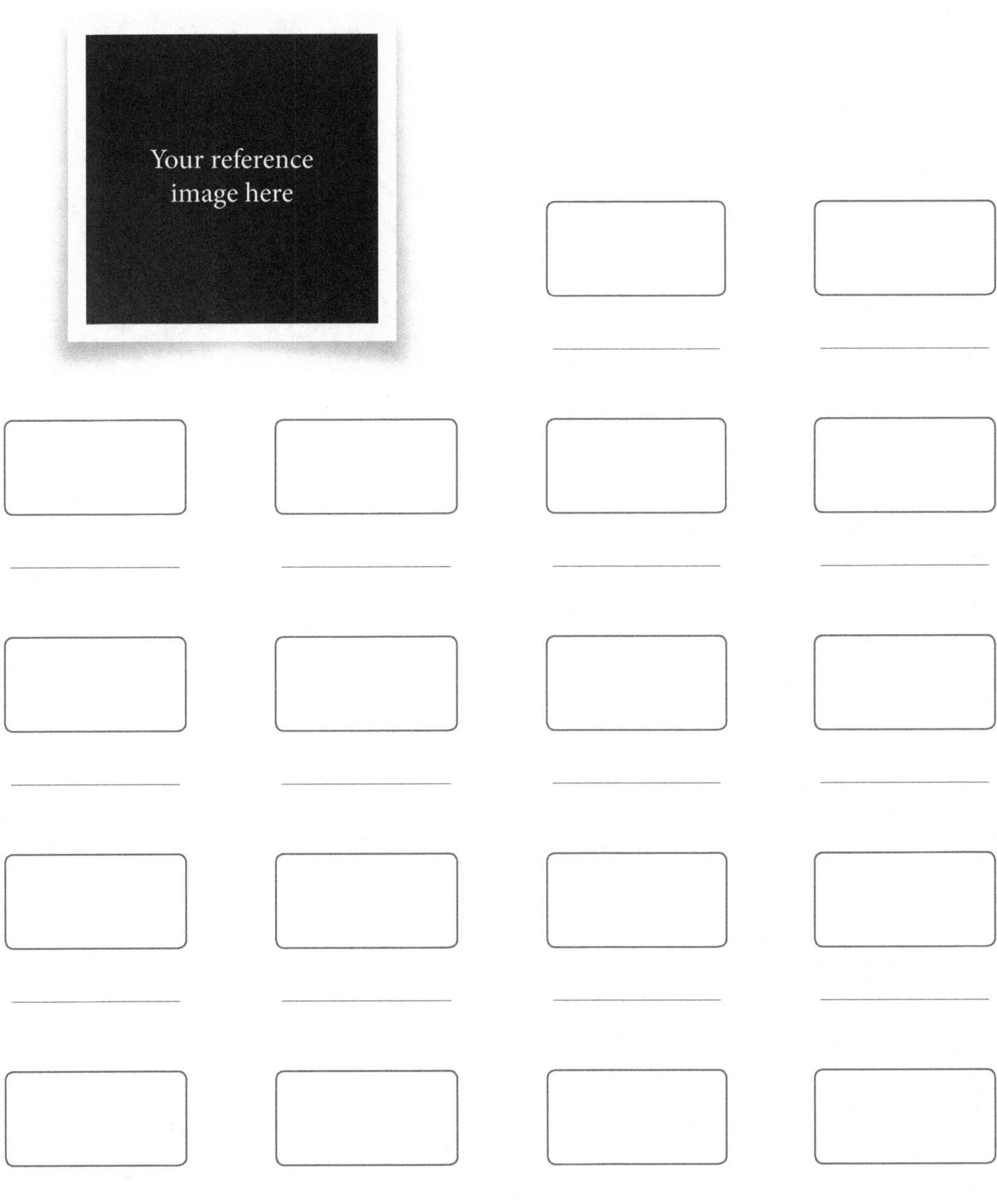

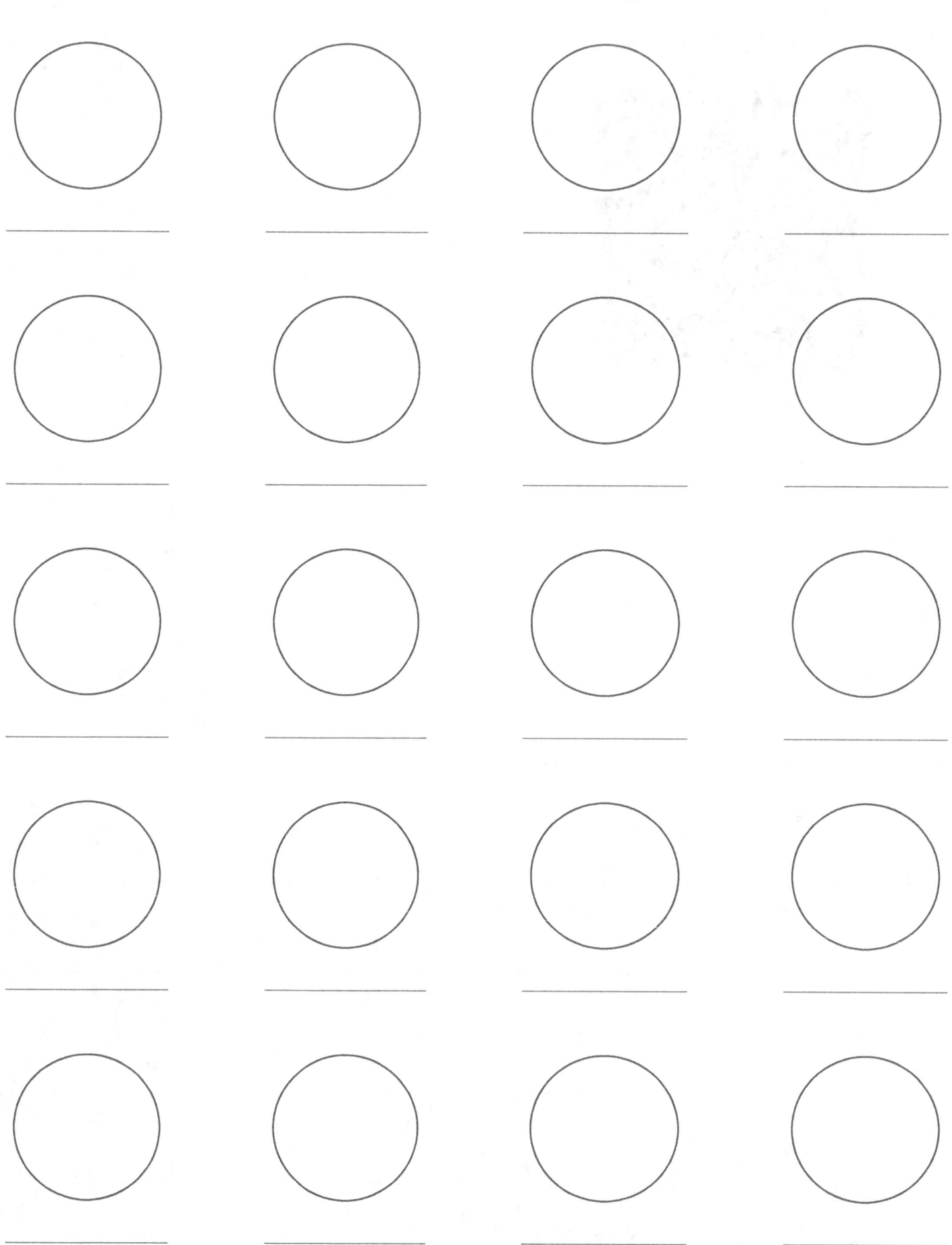

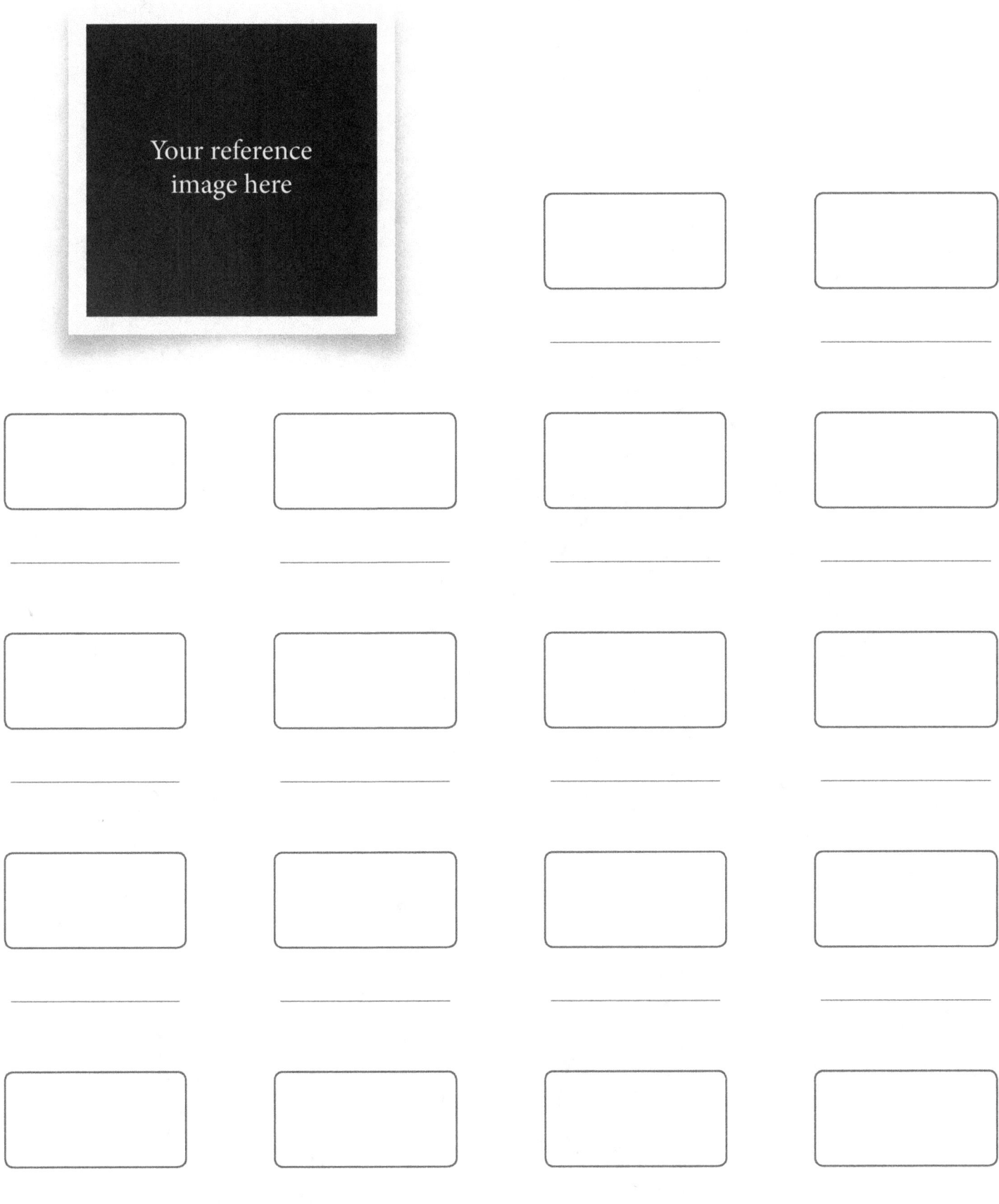

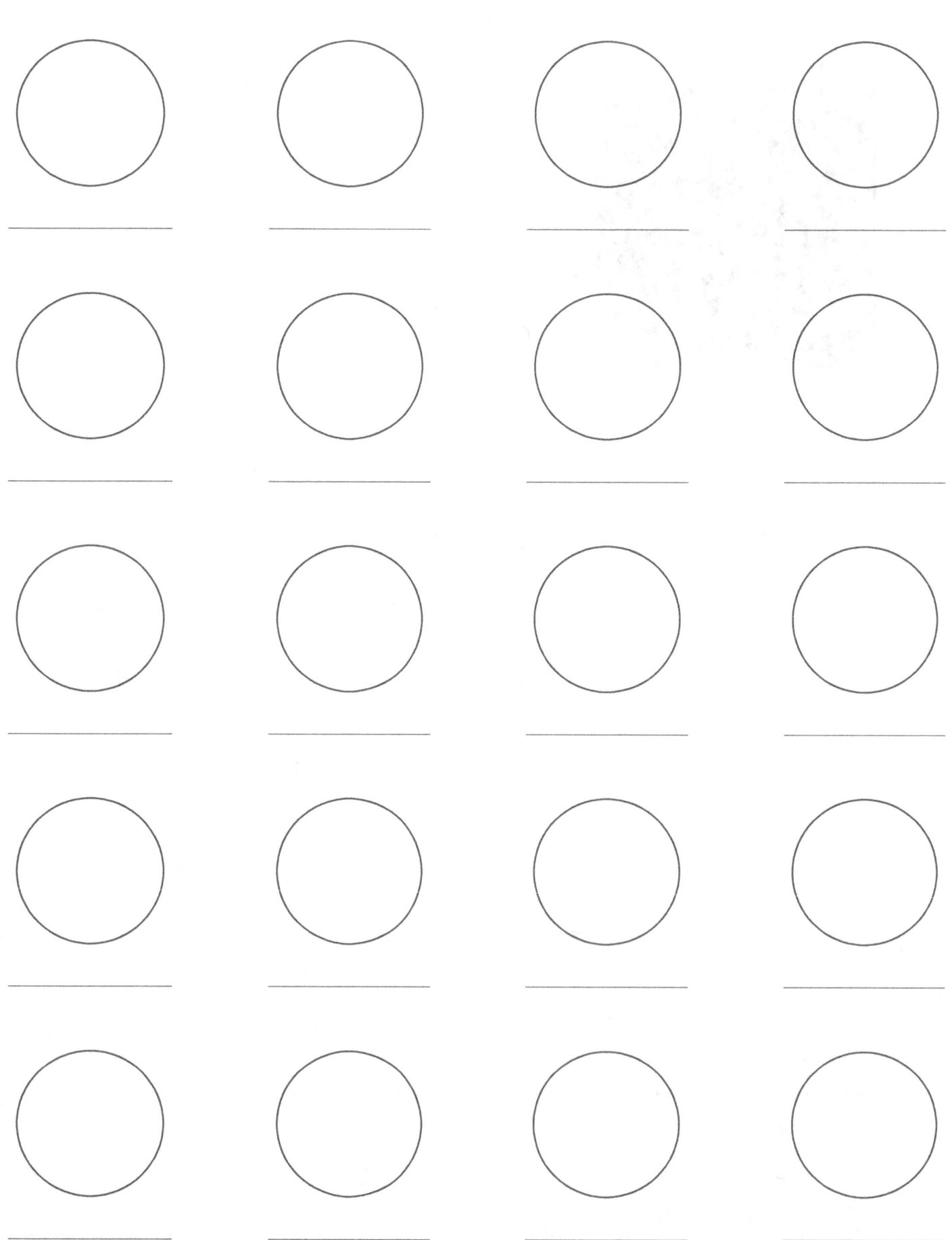

Your reference image here

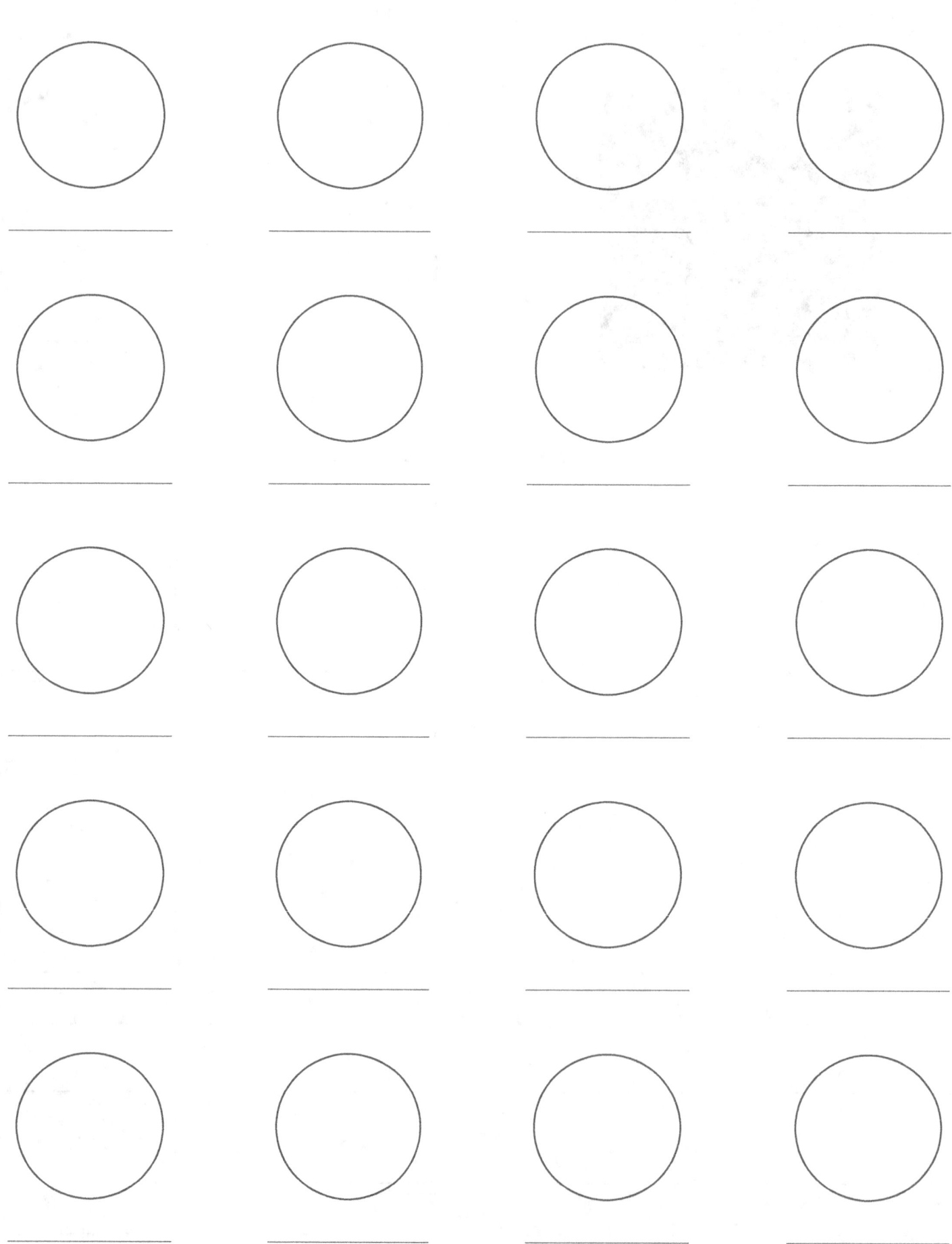

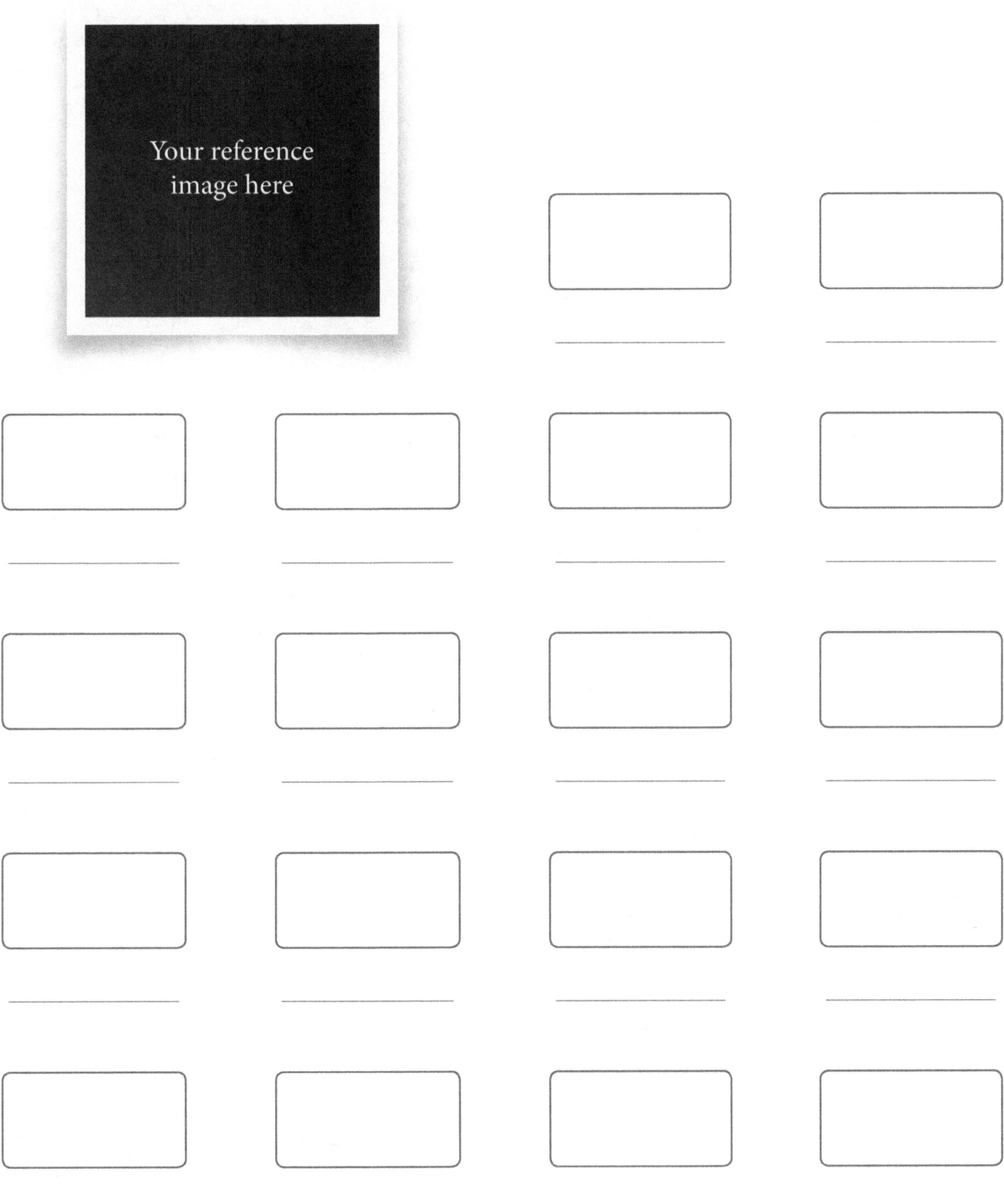

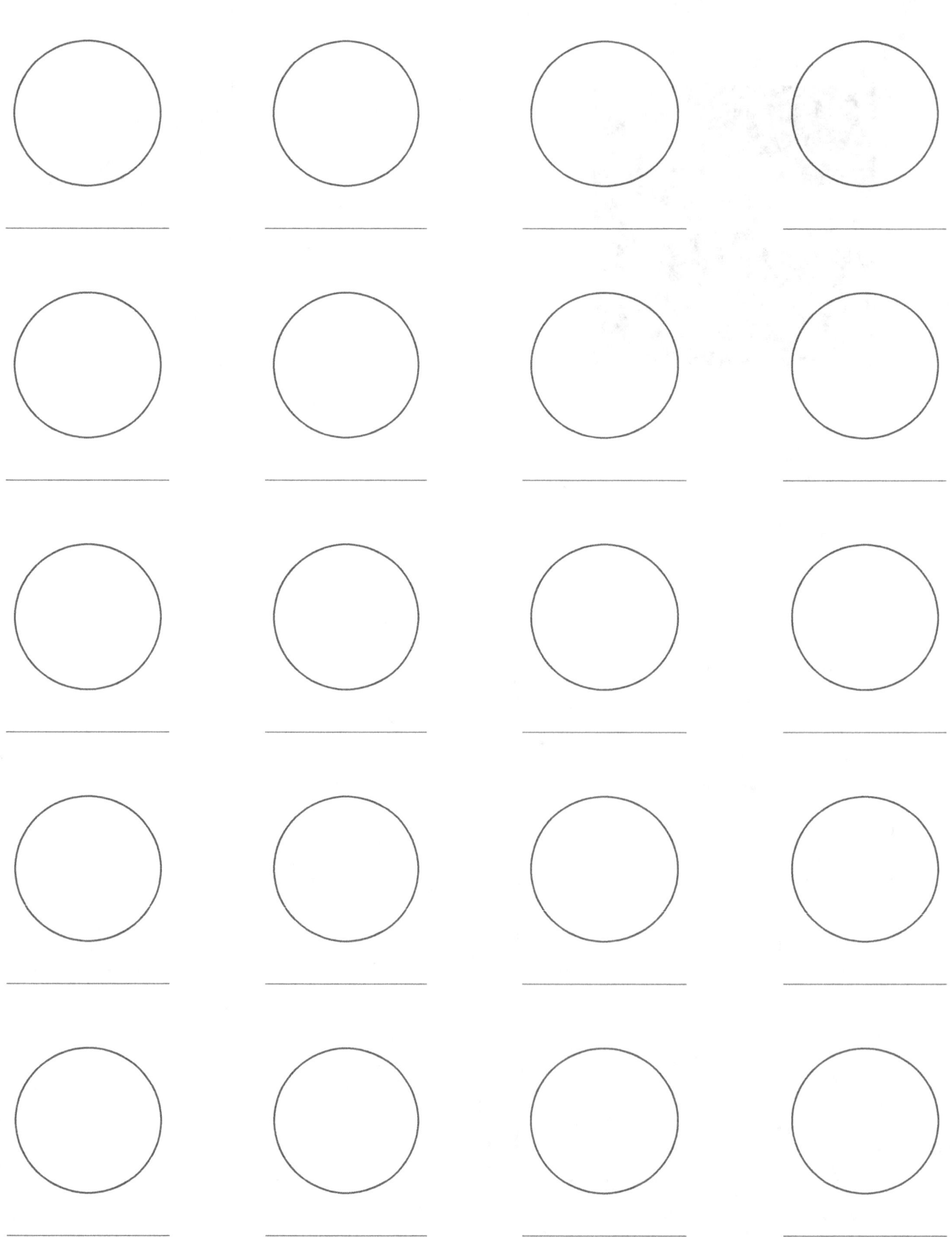

Your reference image here

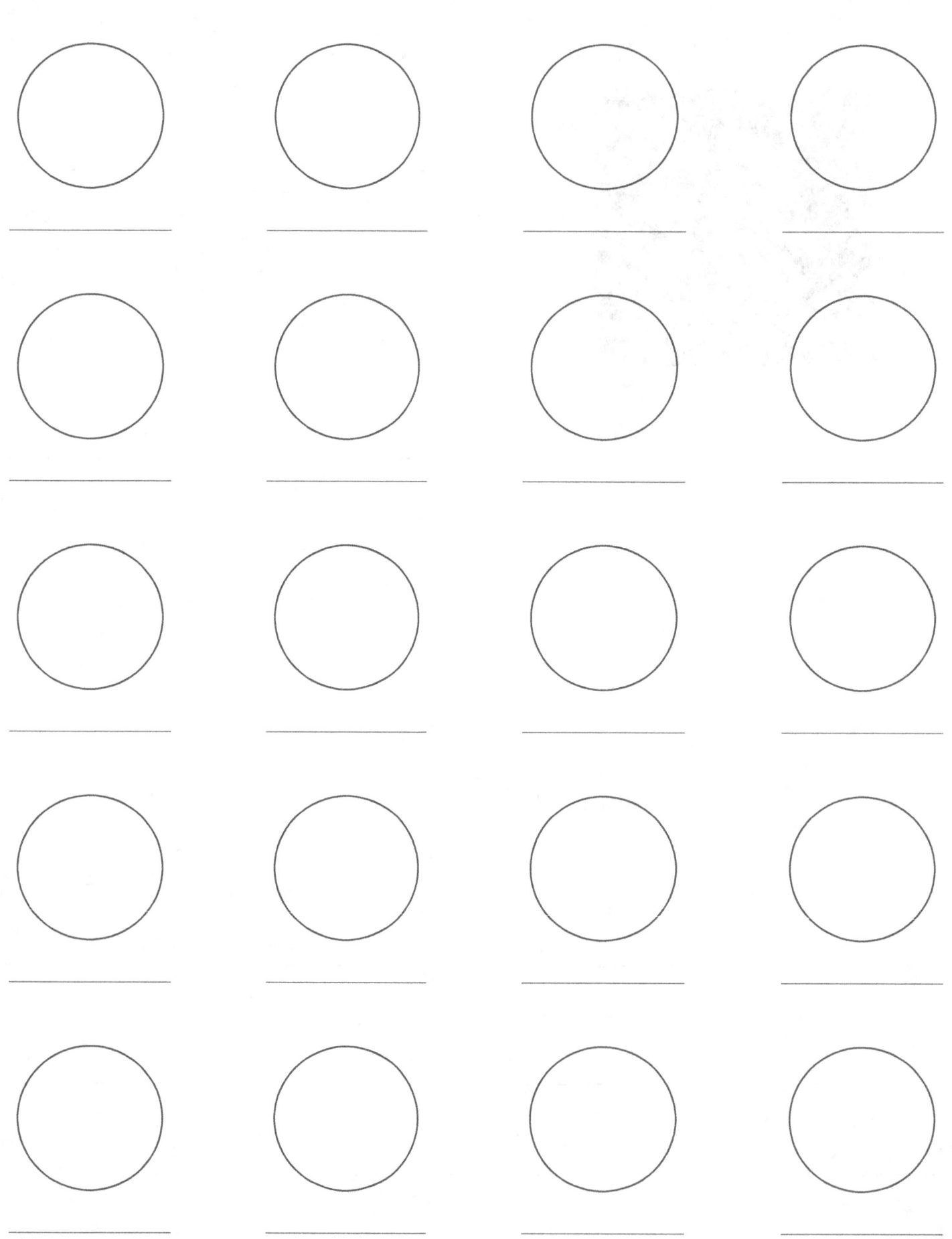

Your reference image here

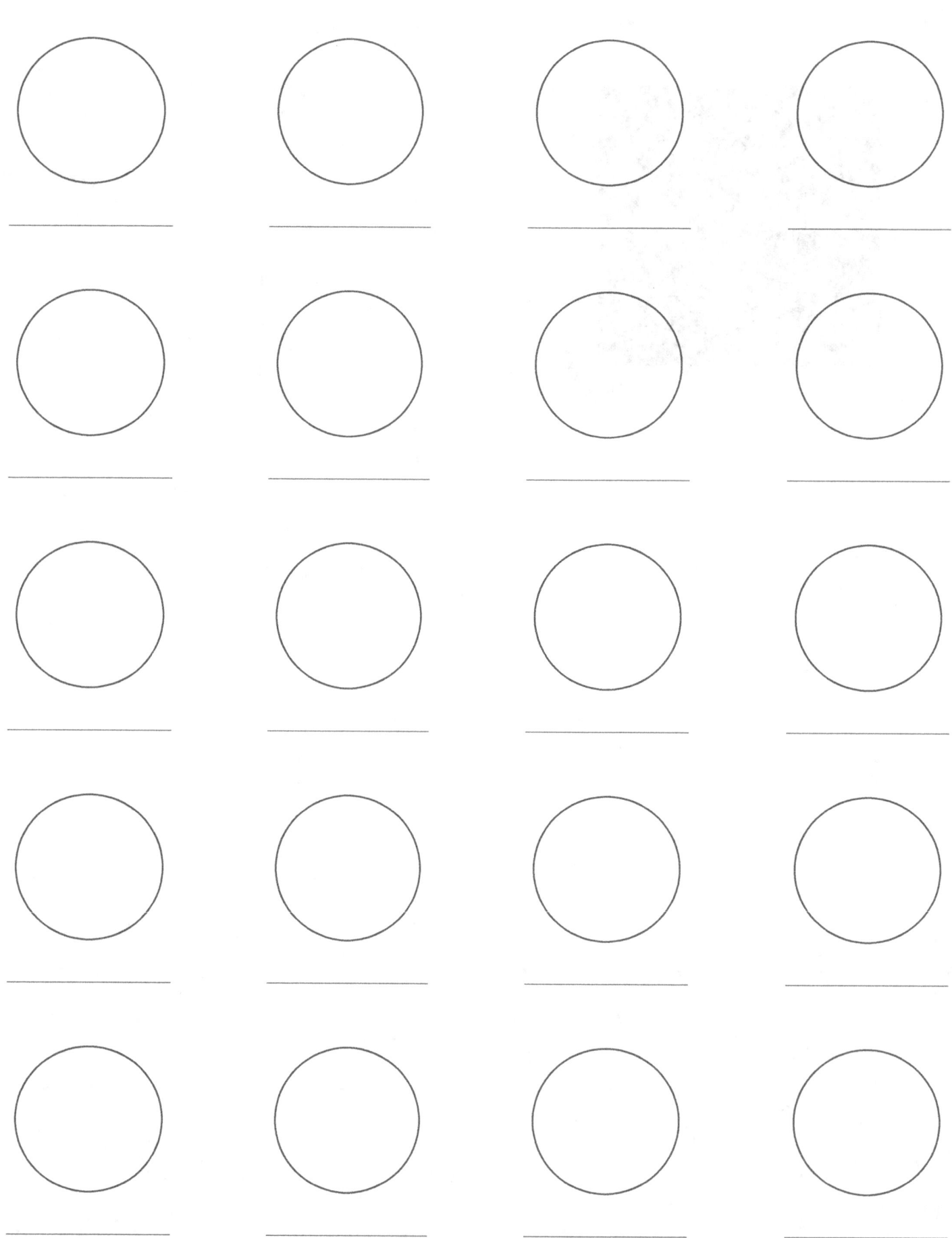

Your reference image here

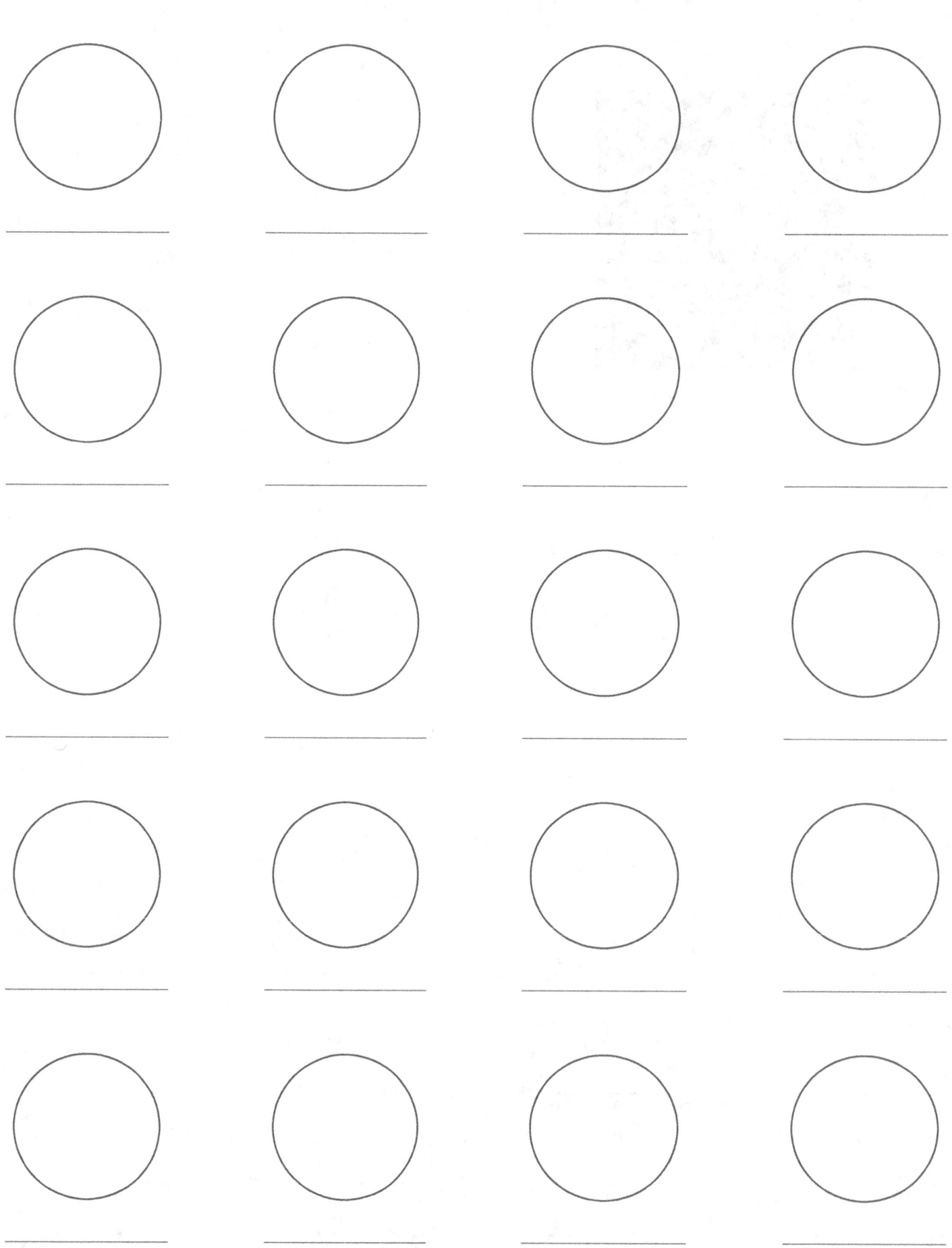

Your reference
image here

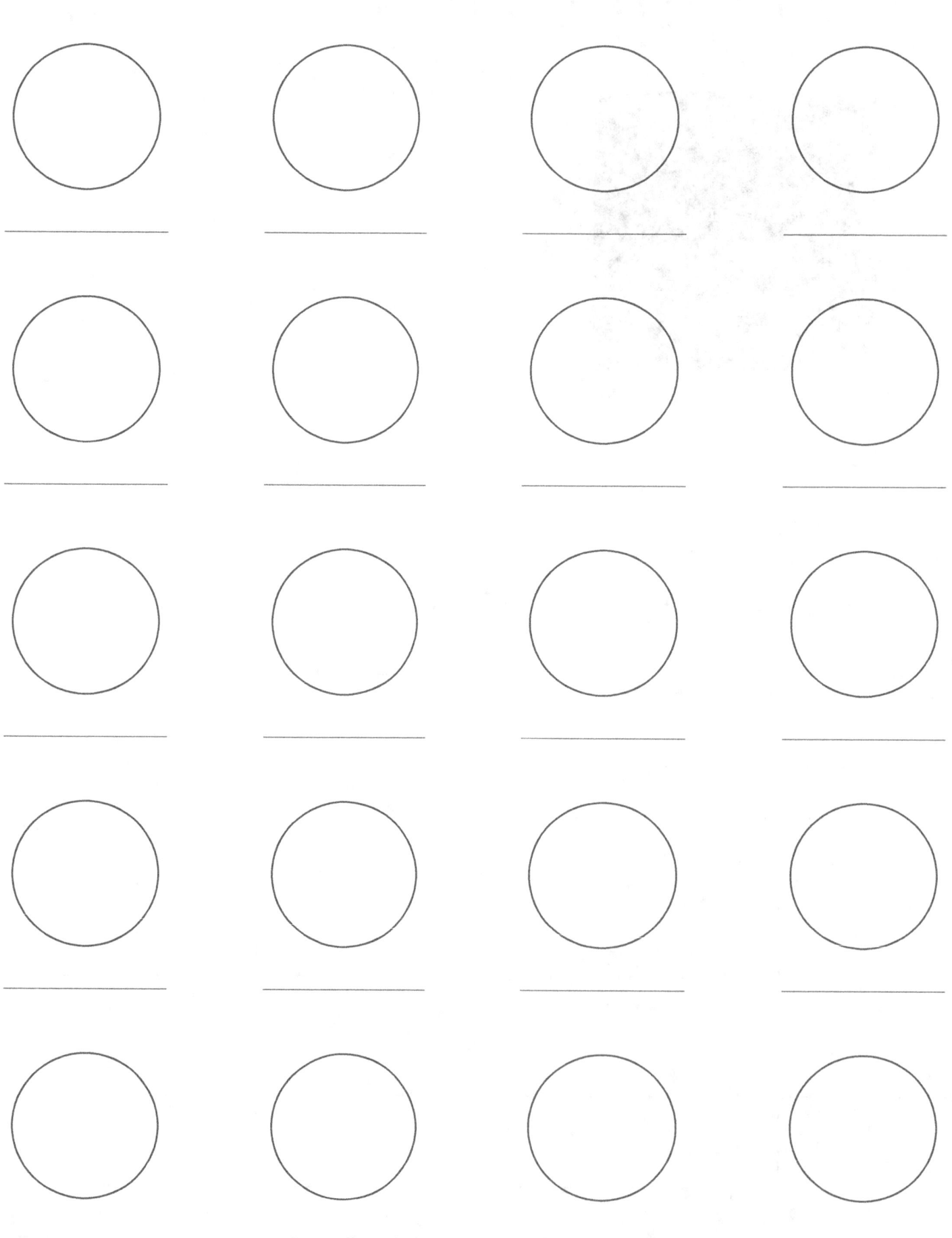

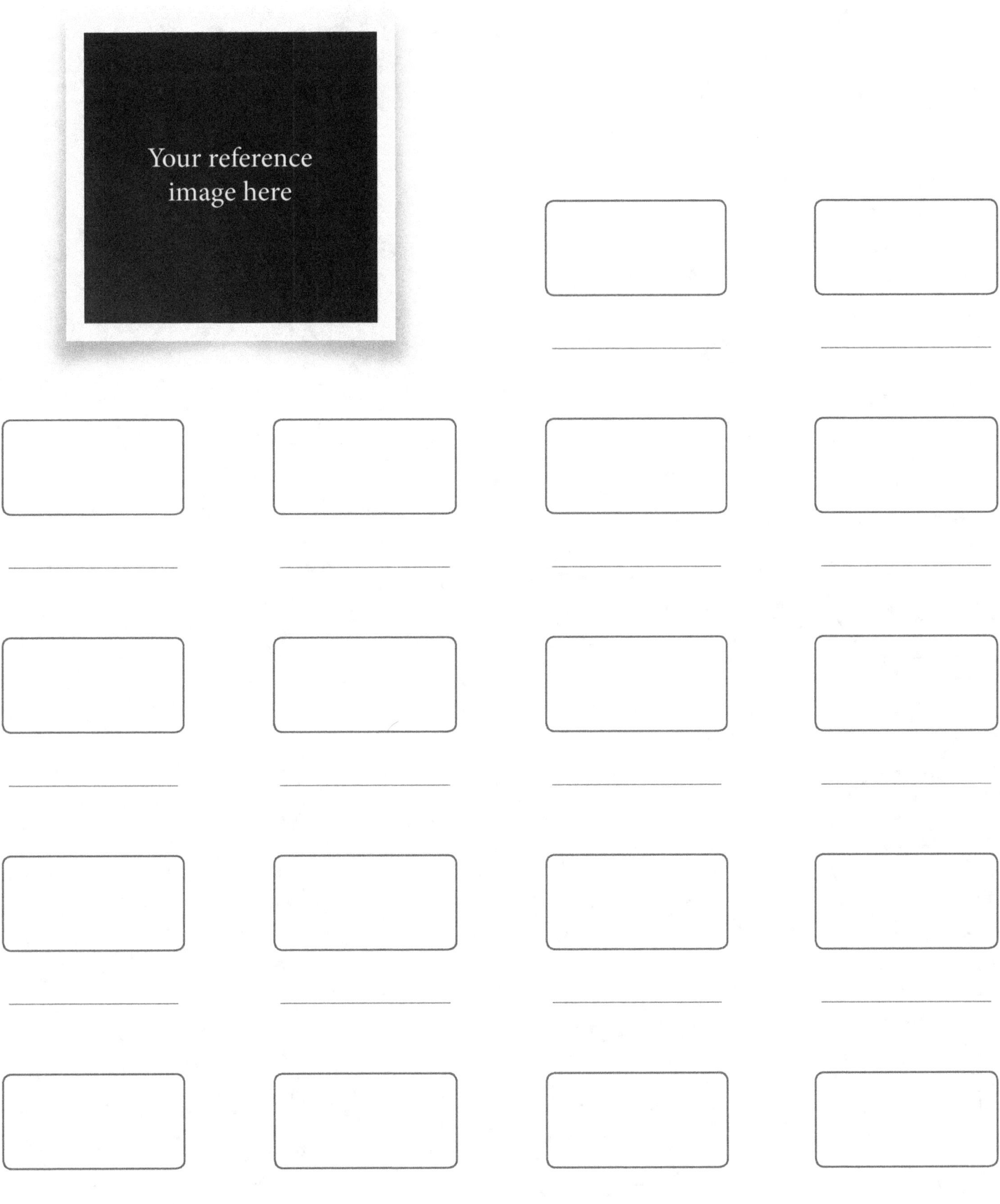

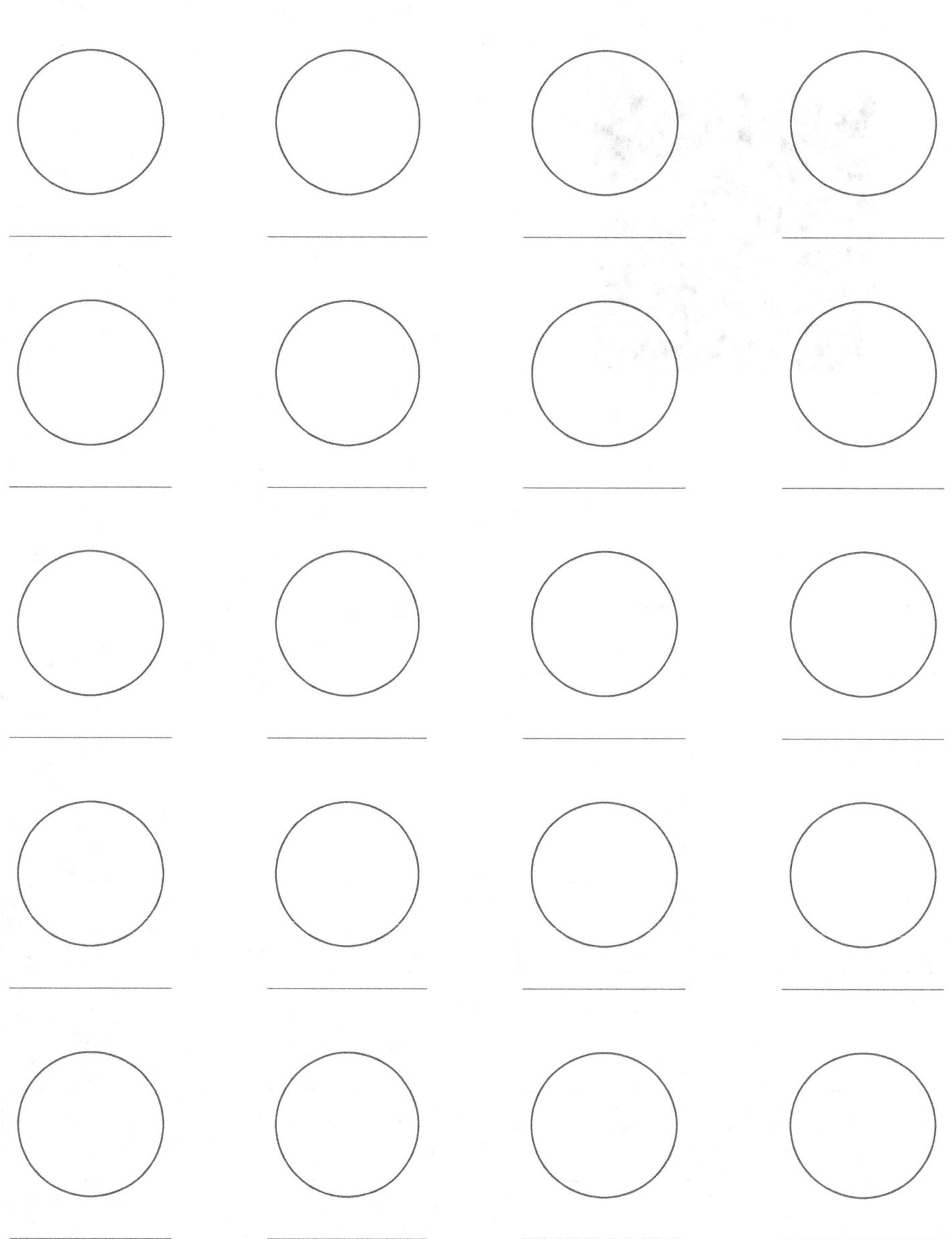

Your reference
image here

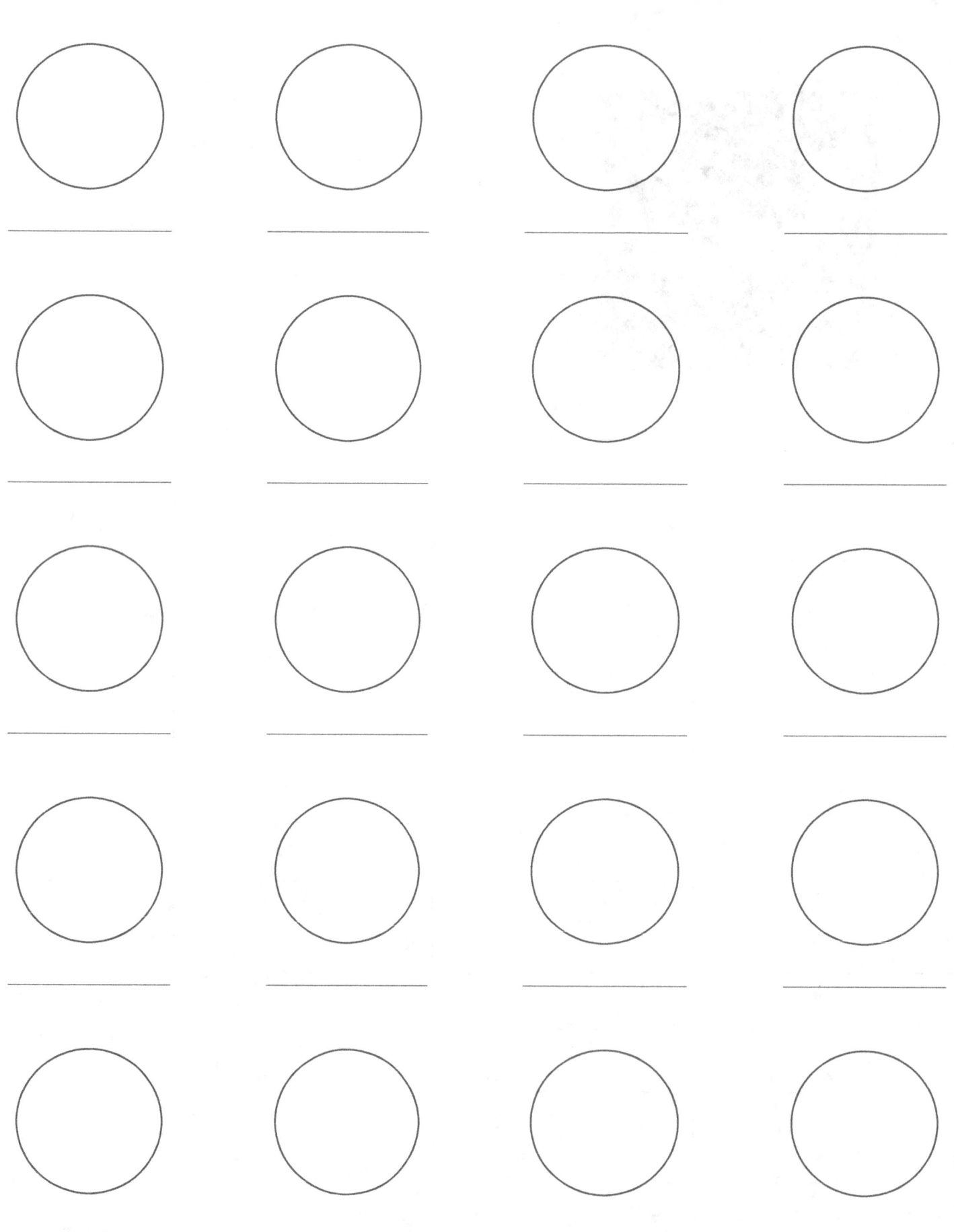

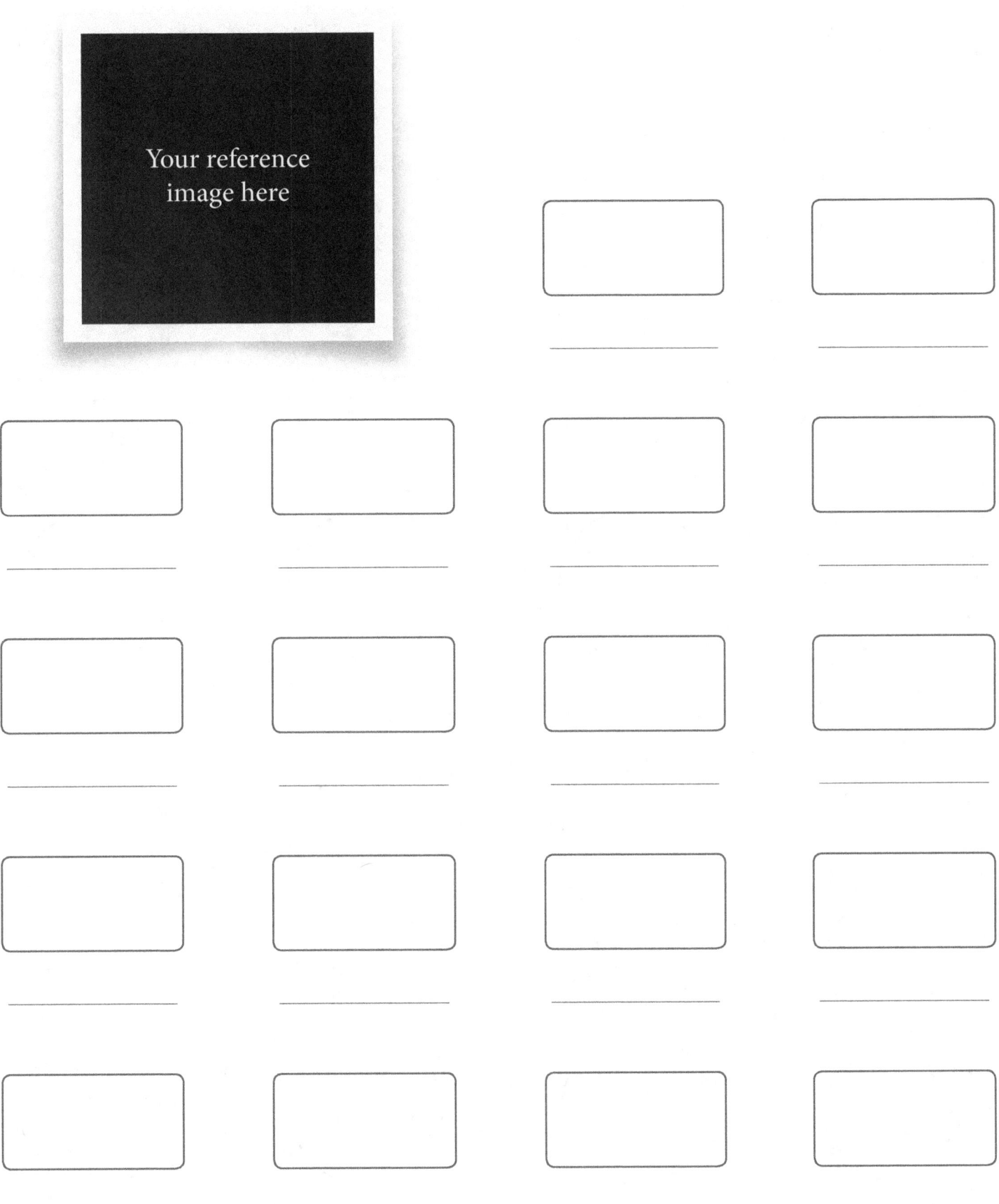

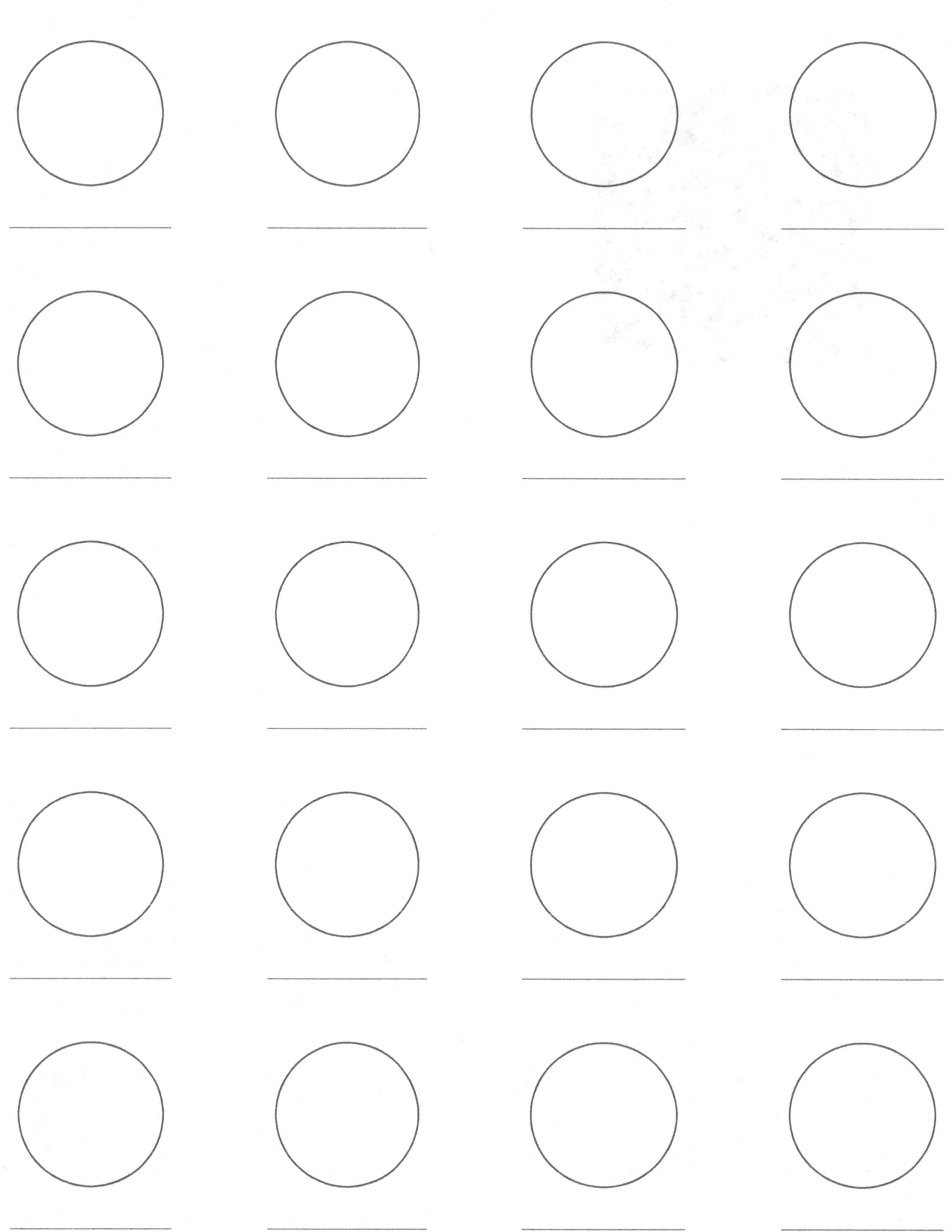

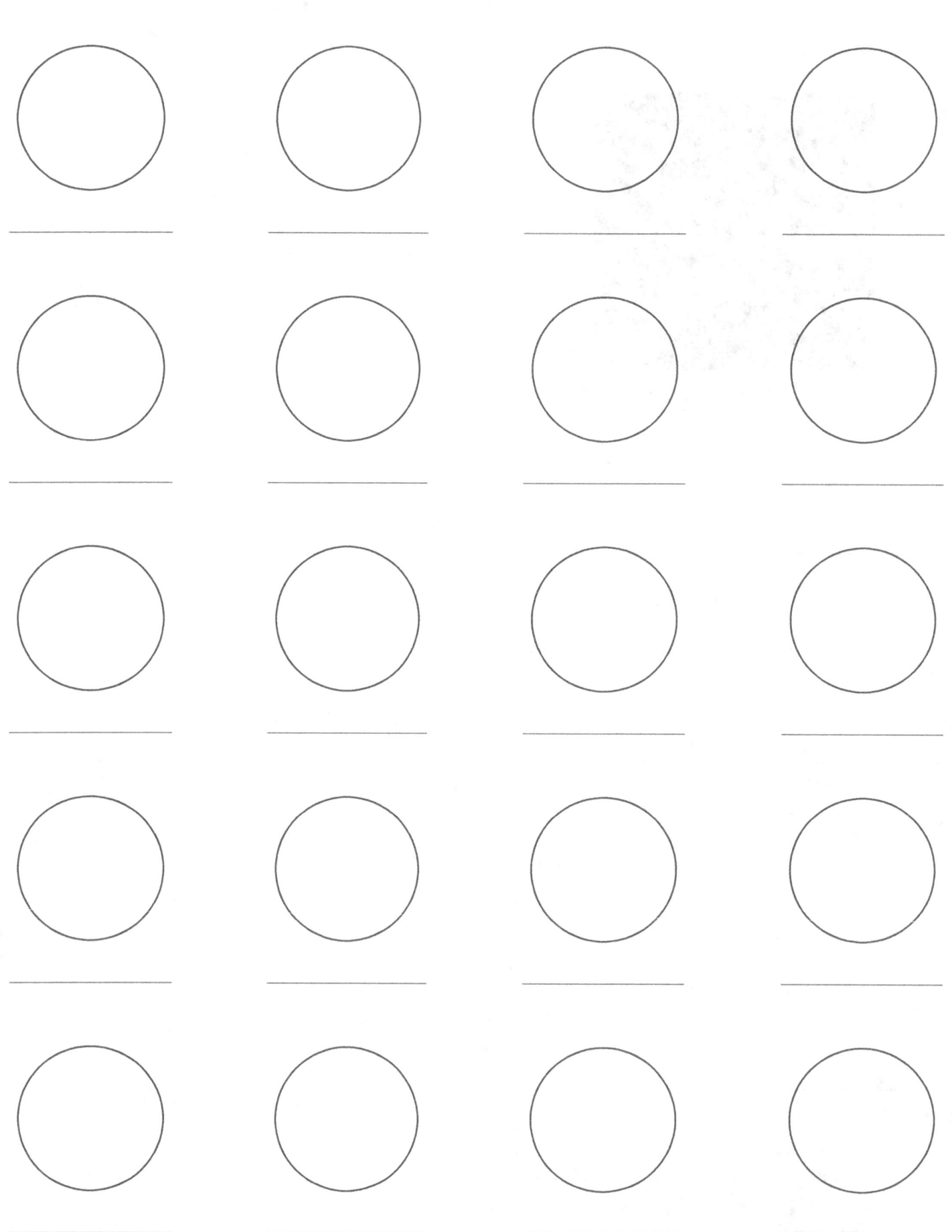

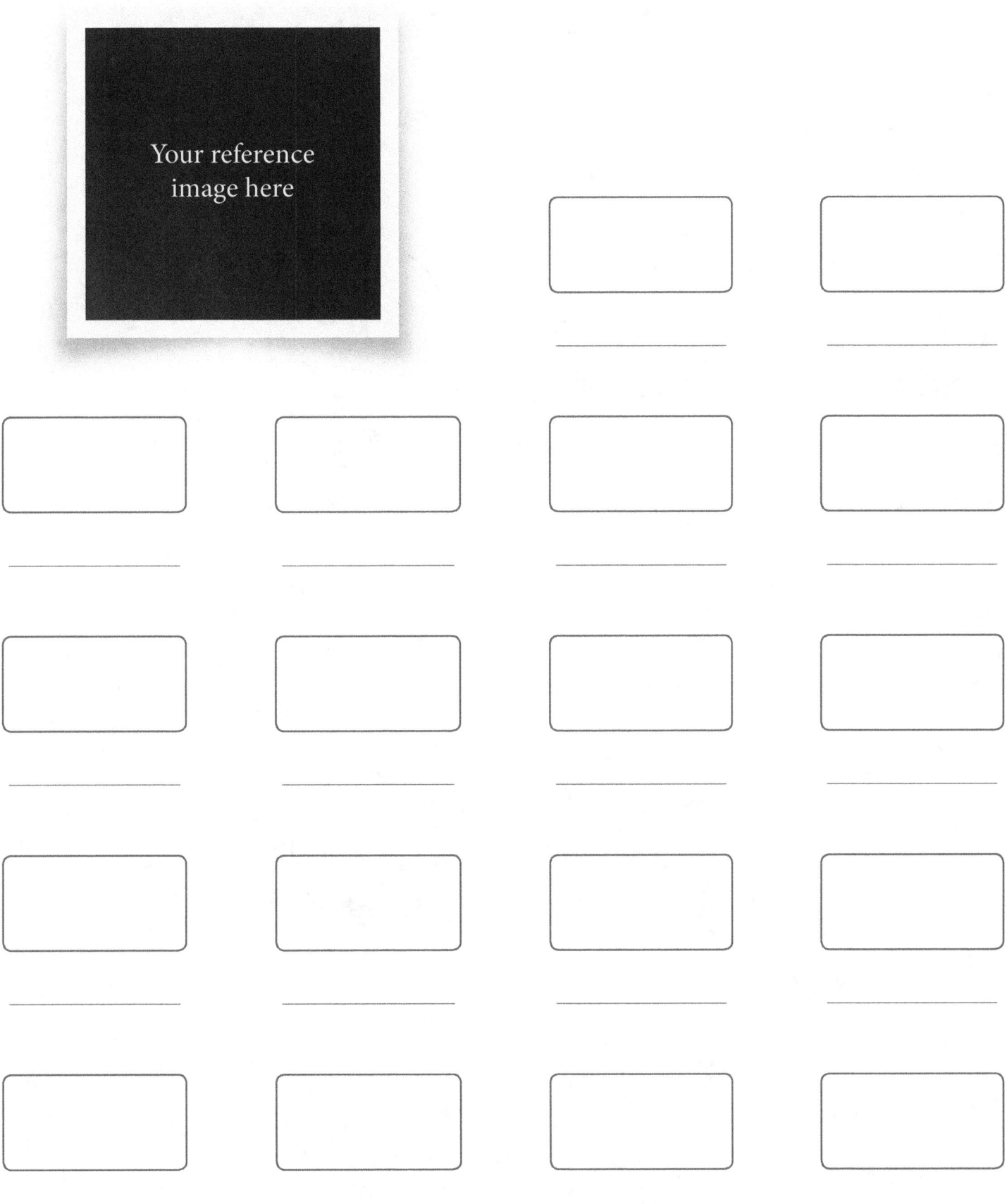

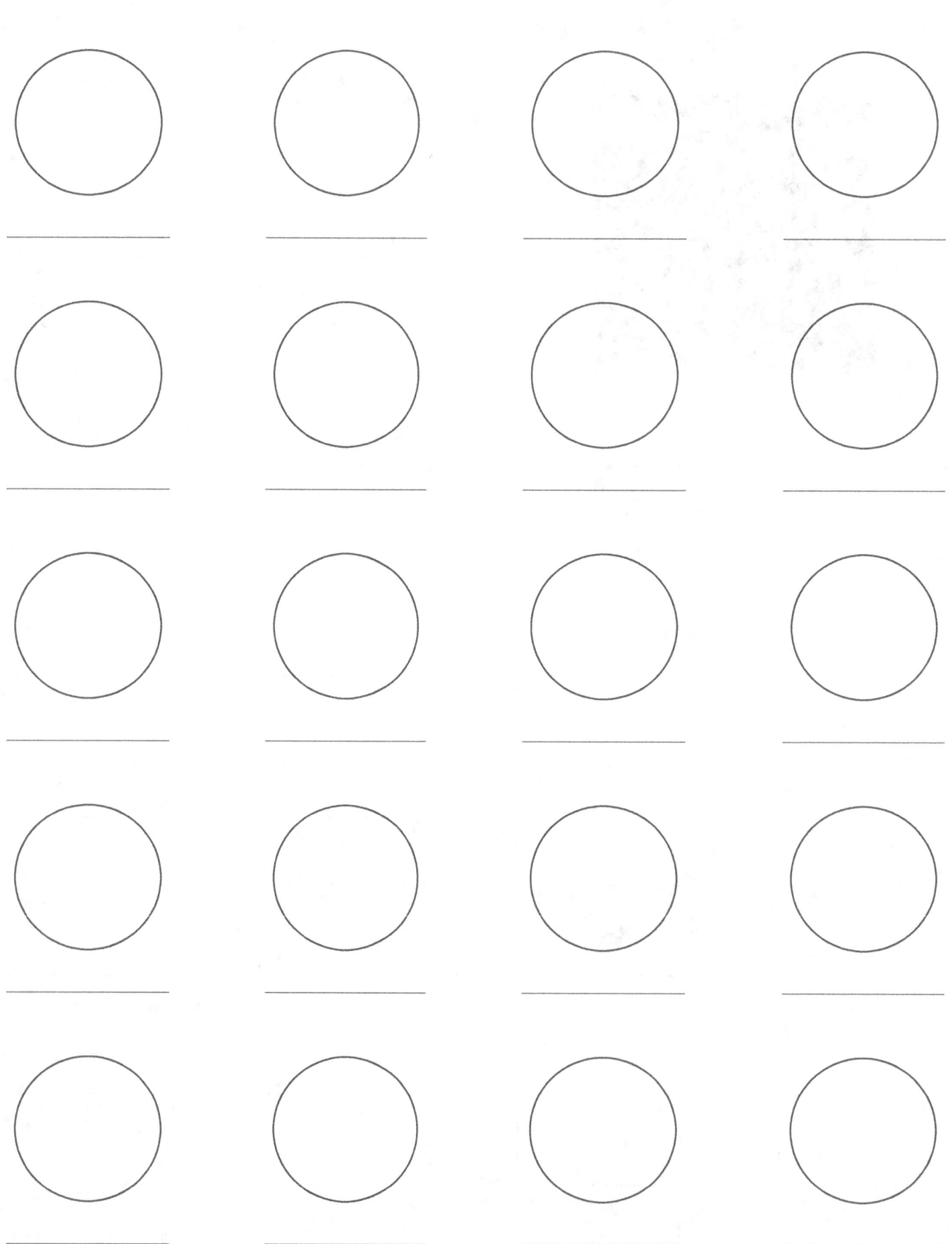

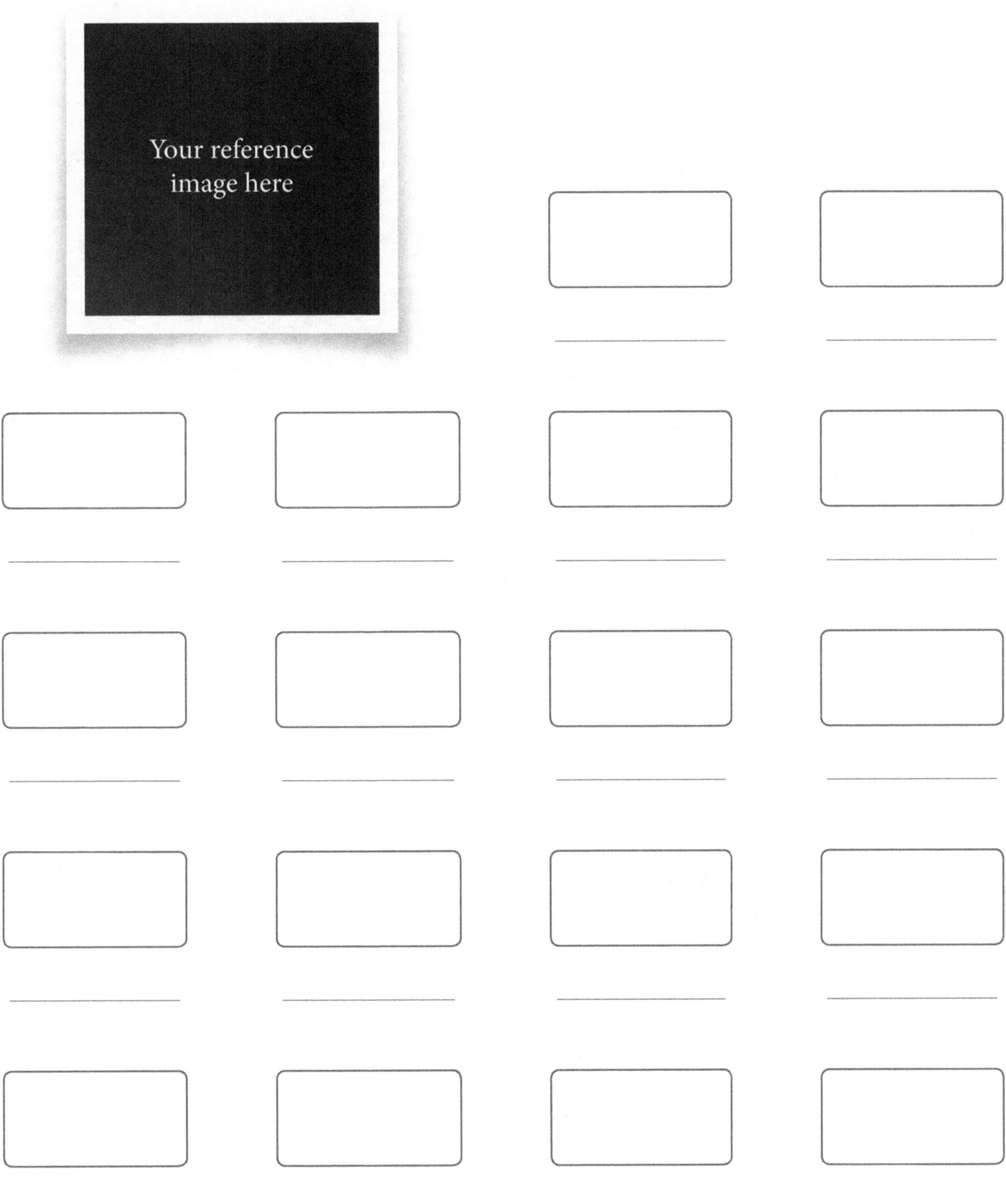

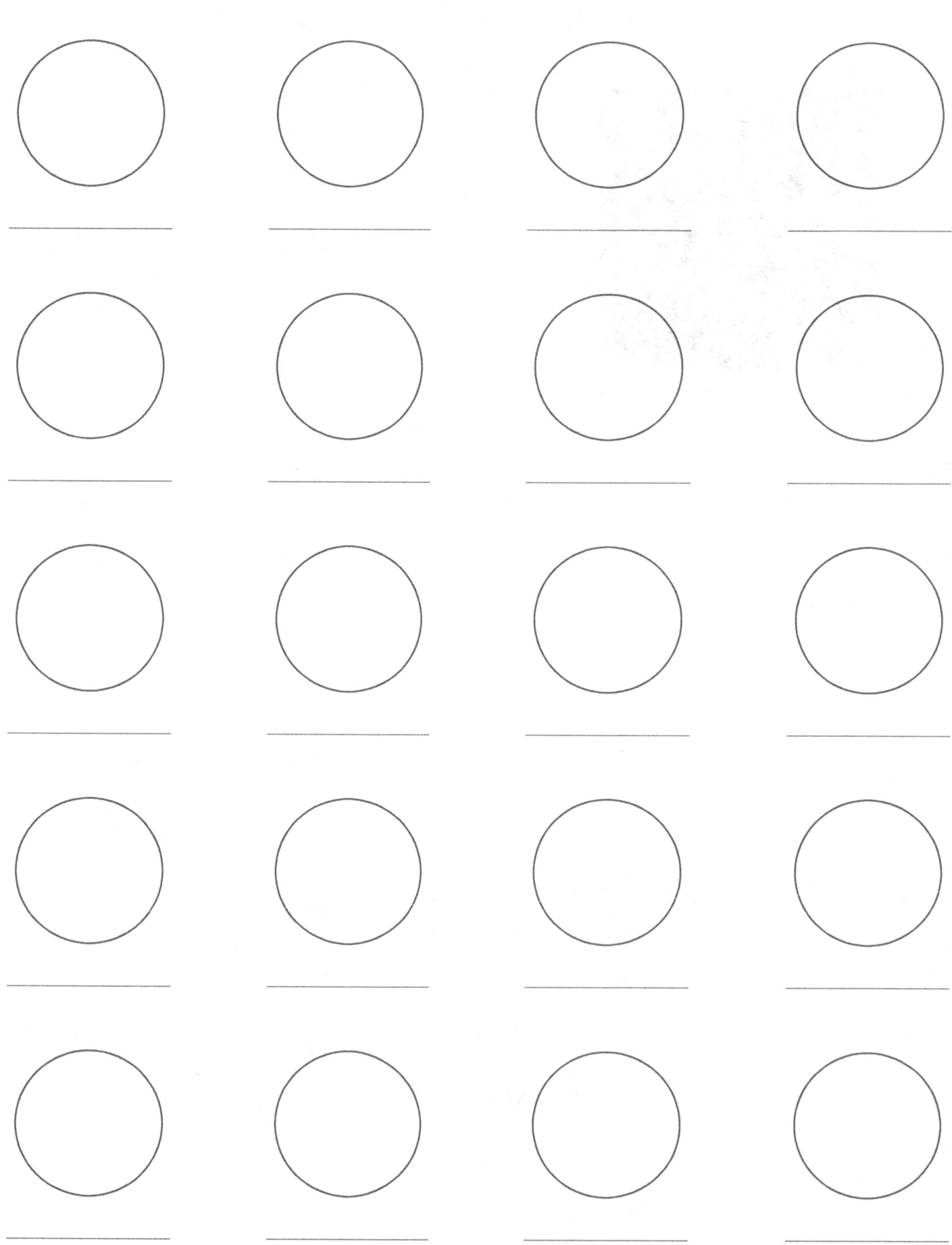

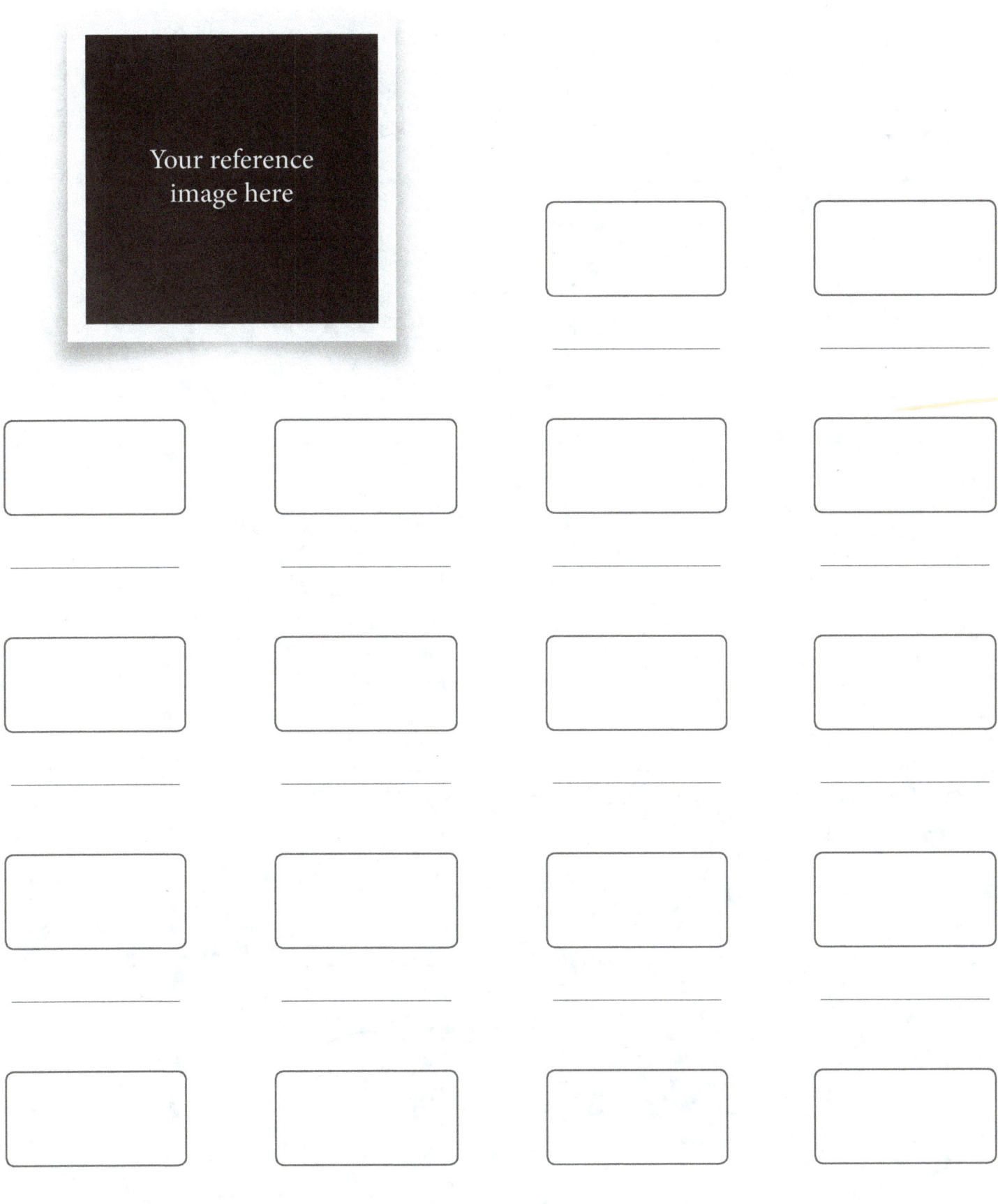

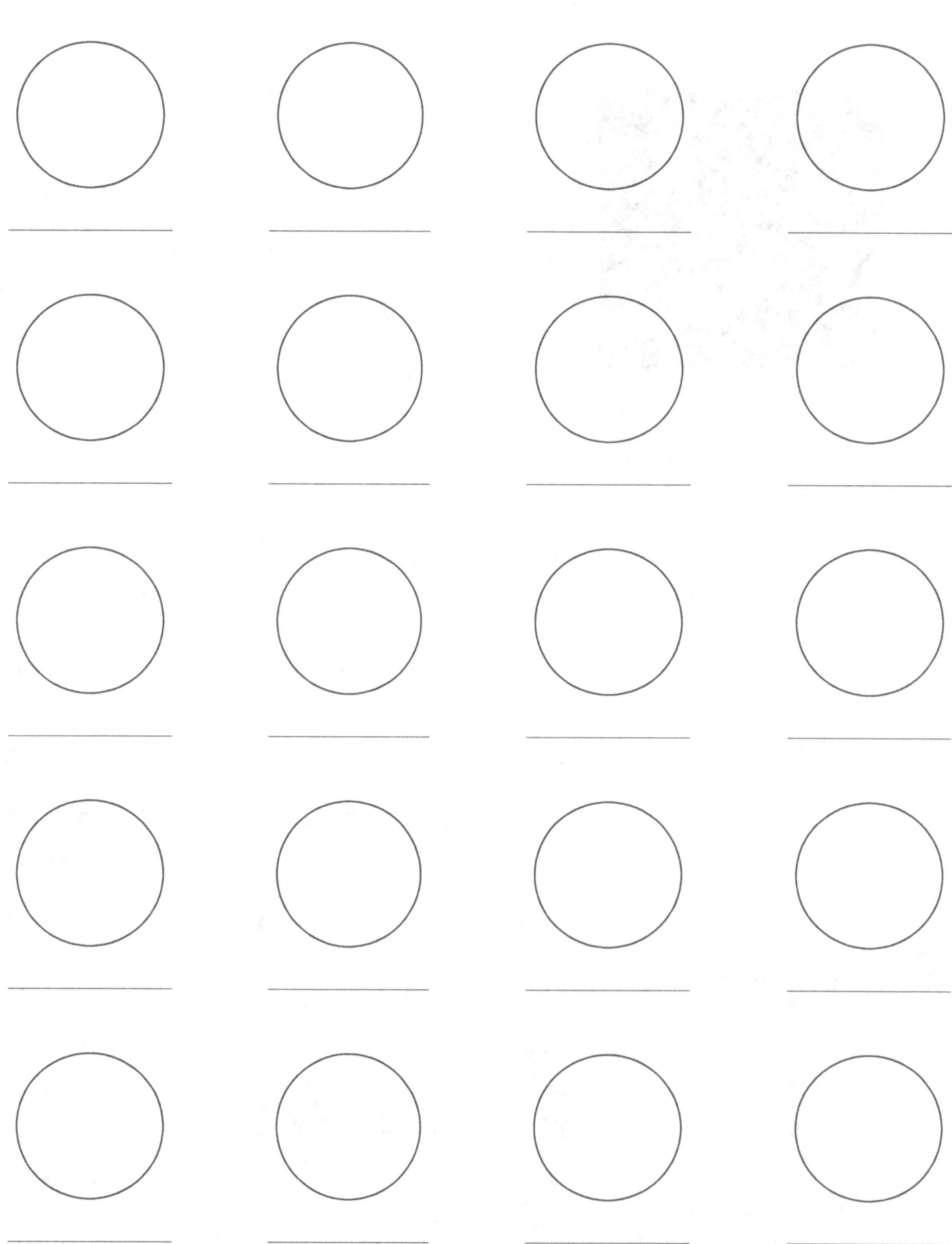

Your reference image here

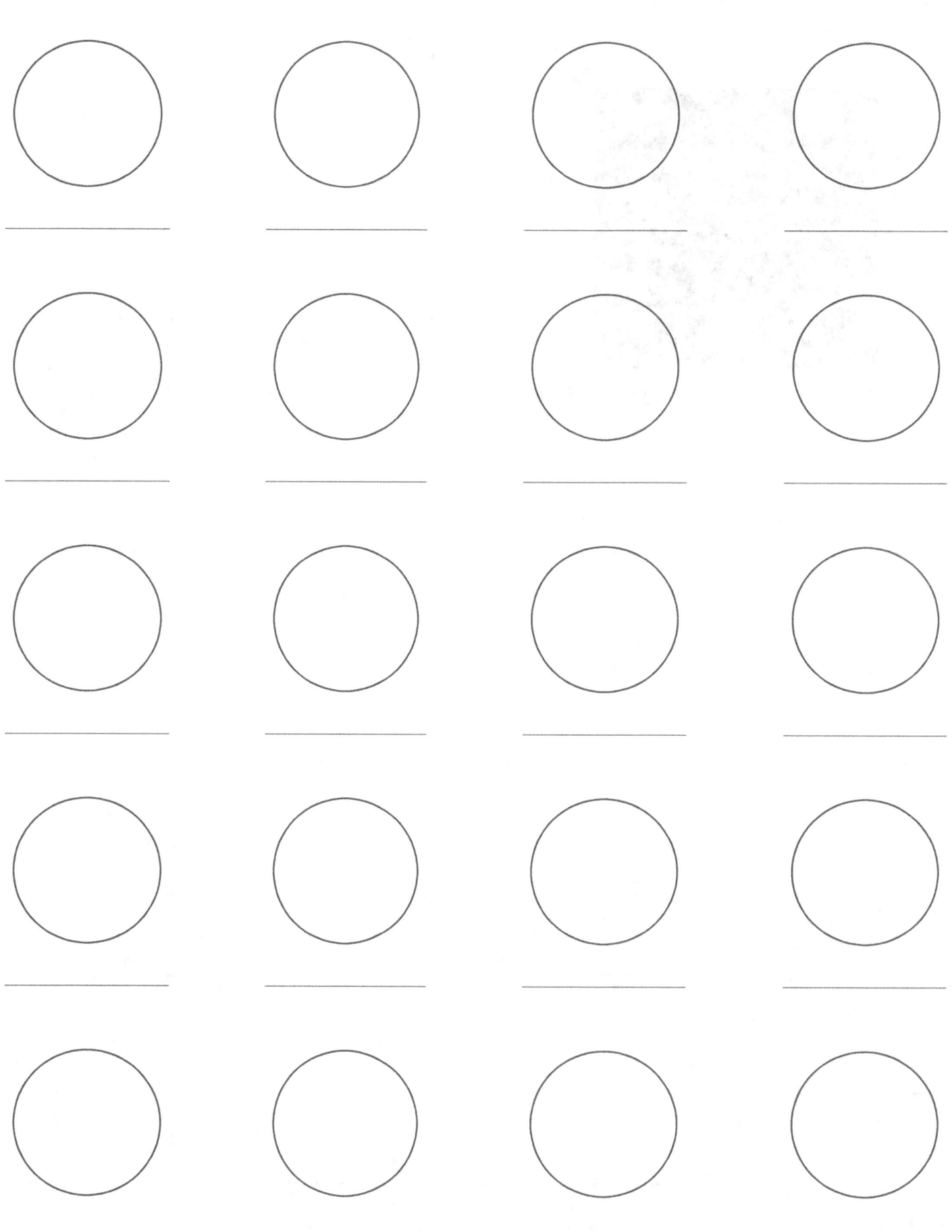

Your reference image here

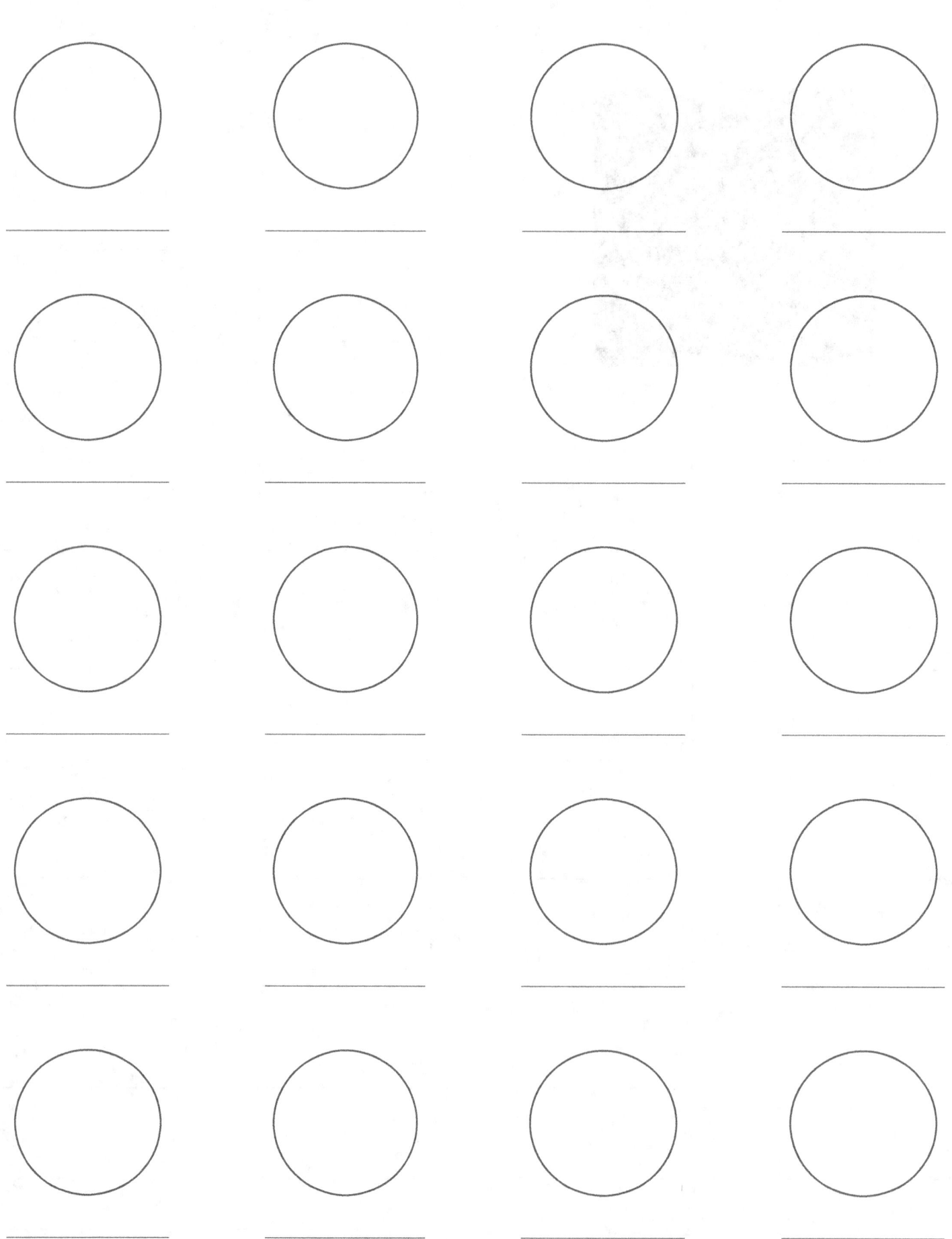

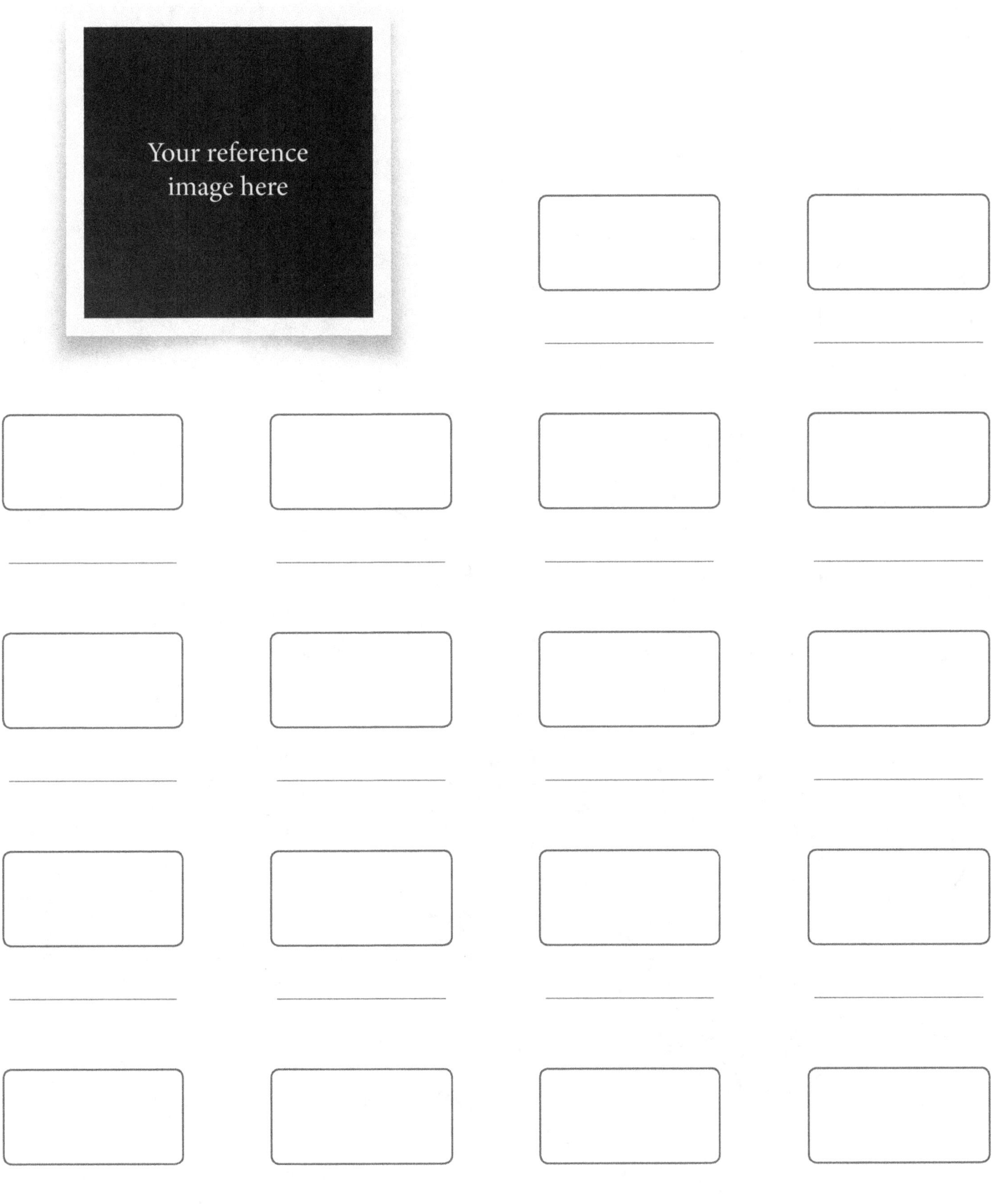

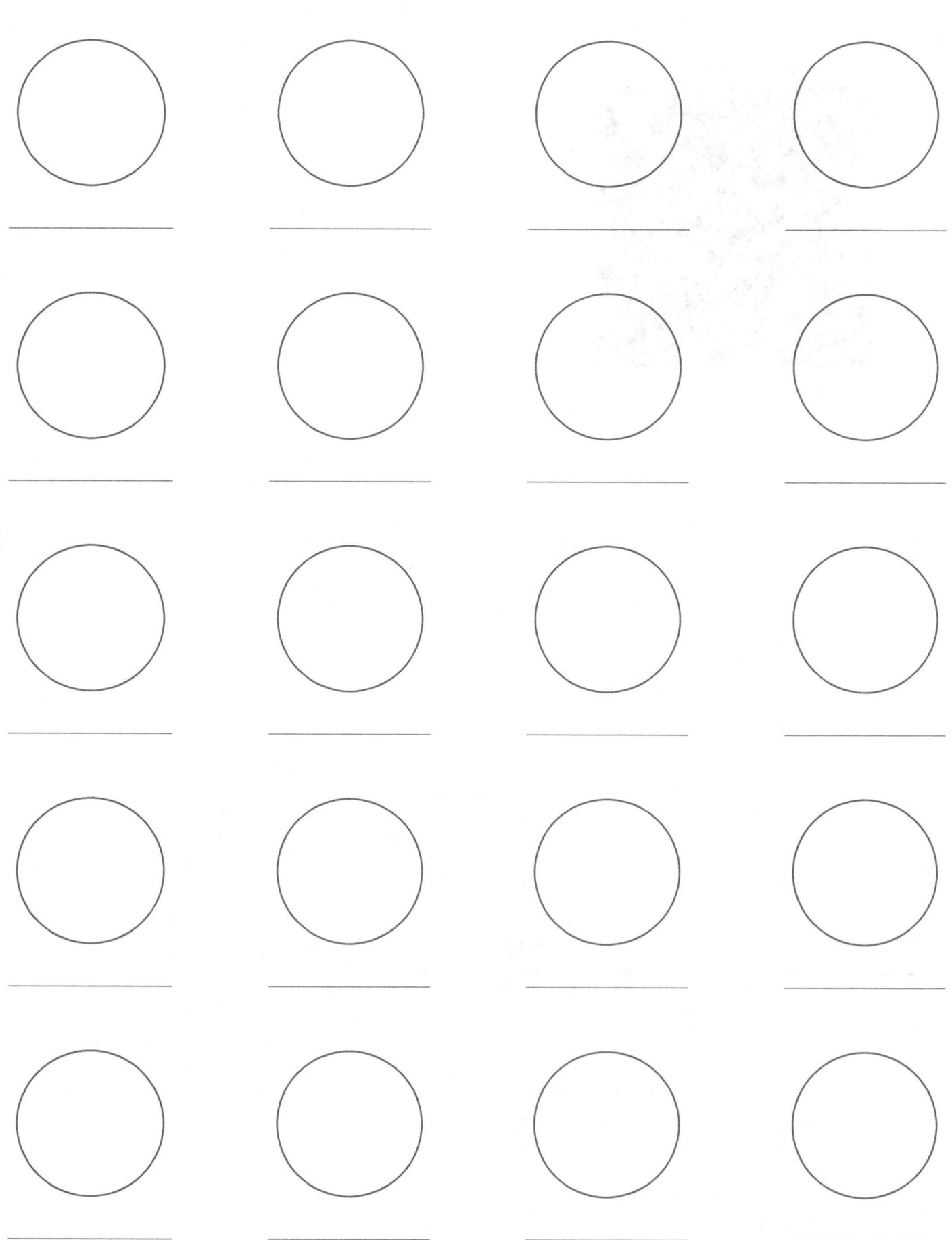

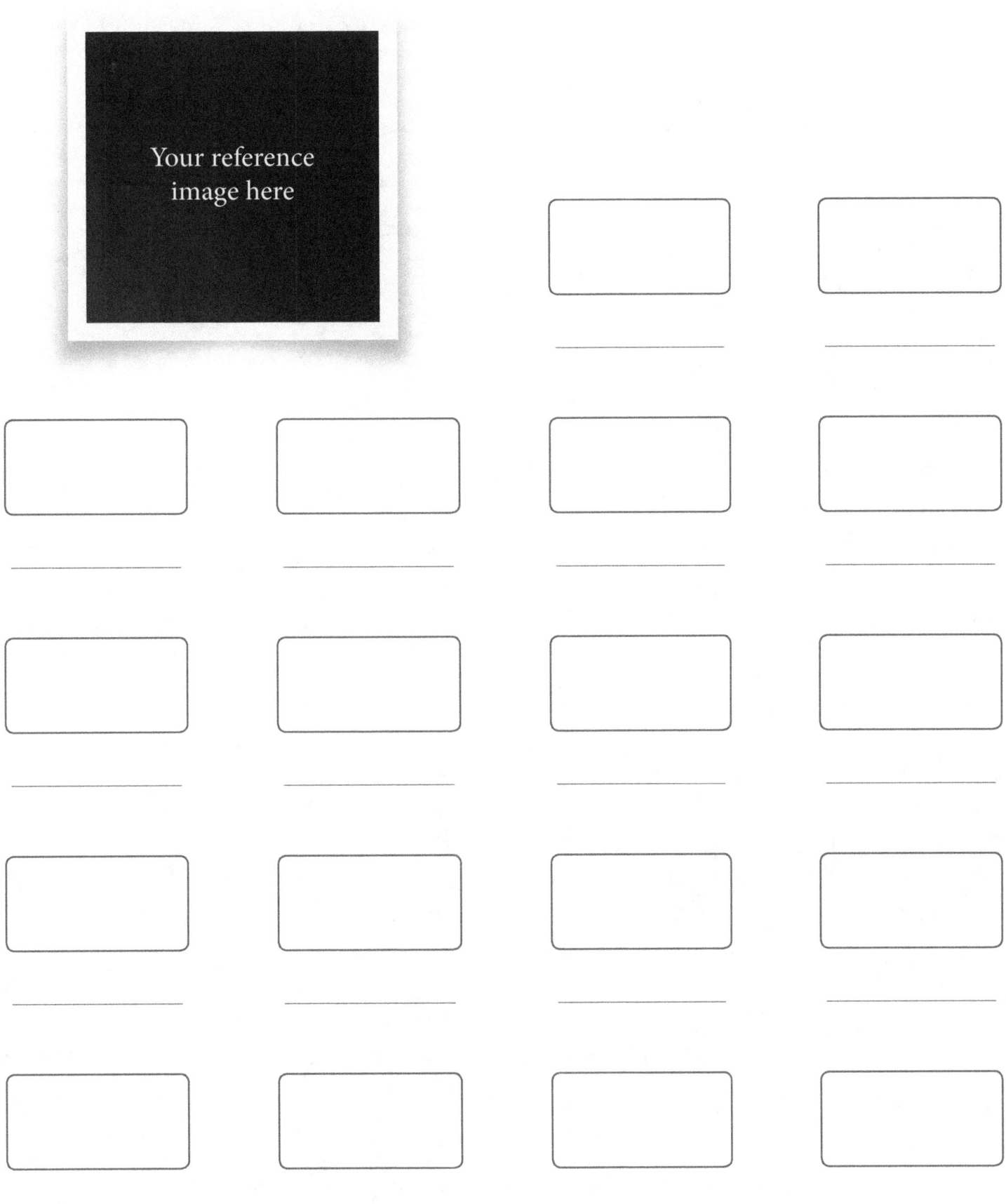

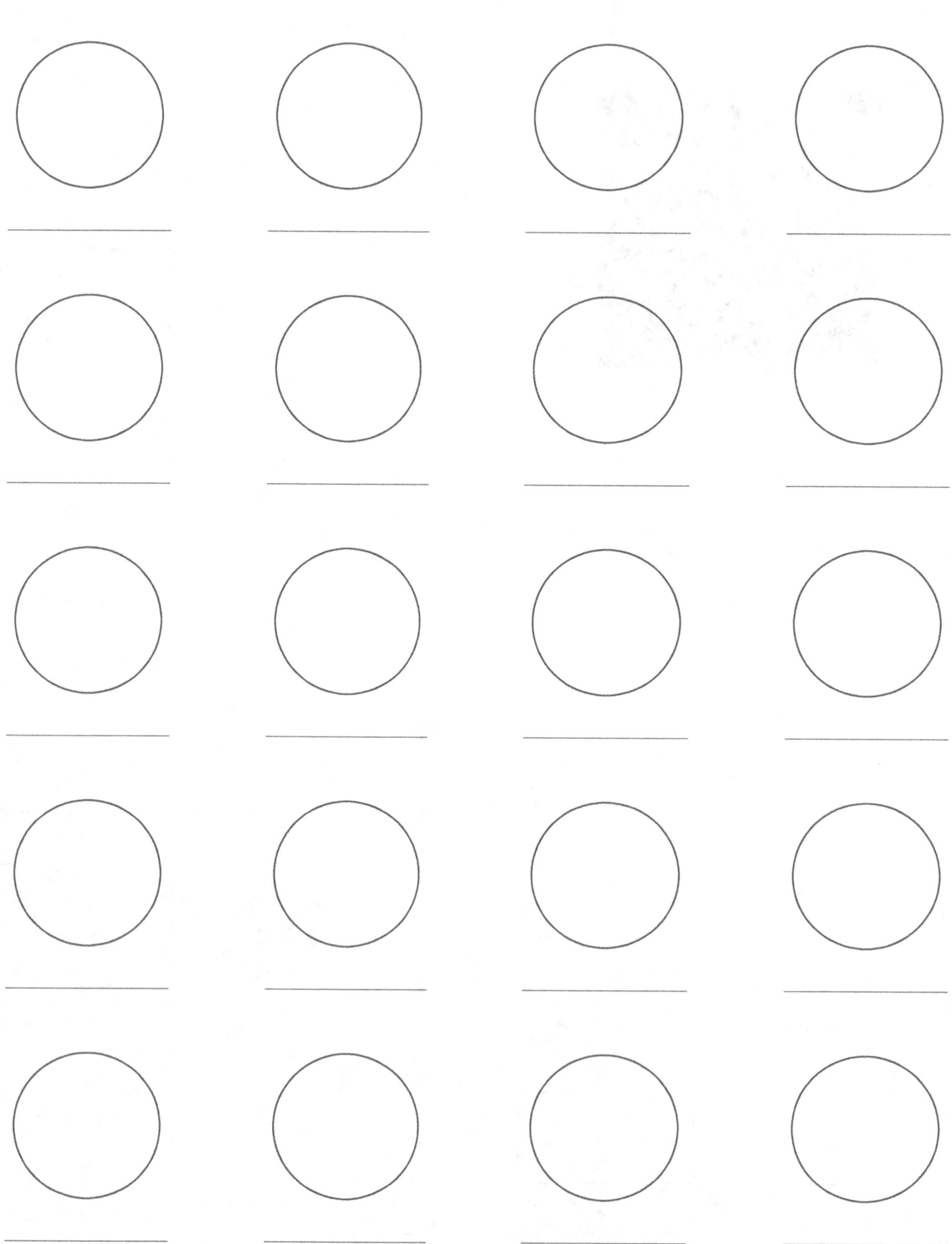

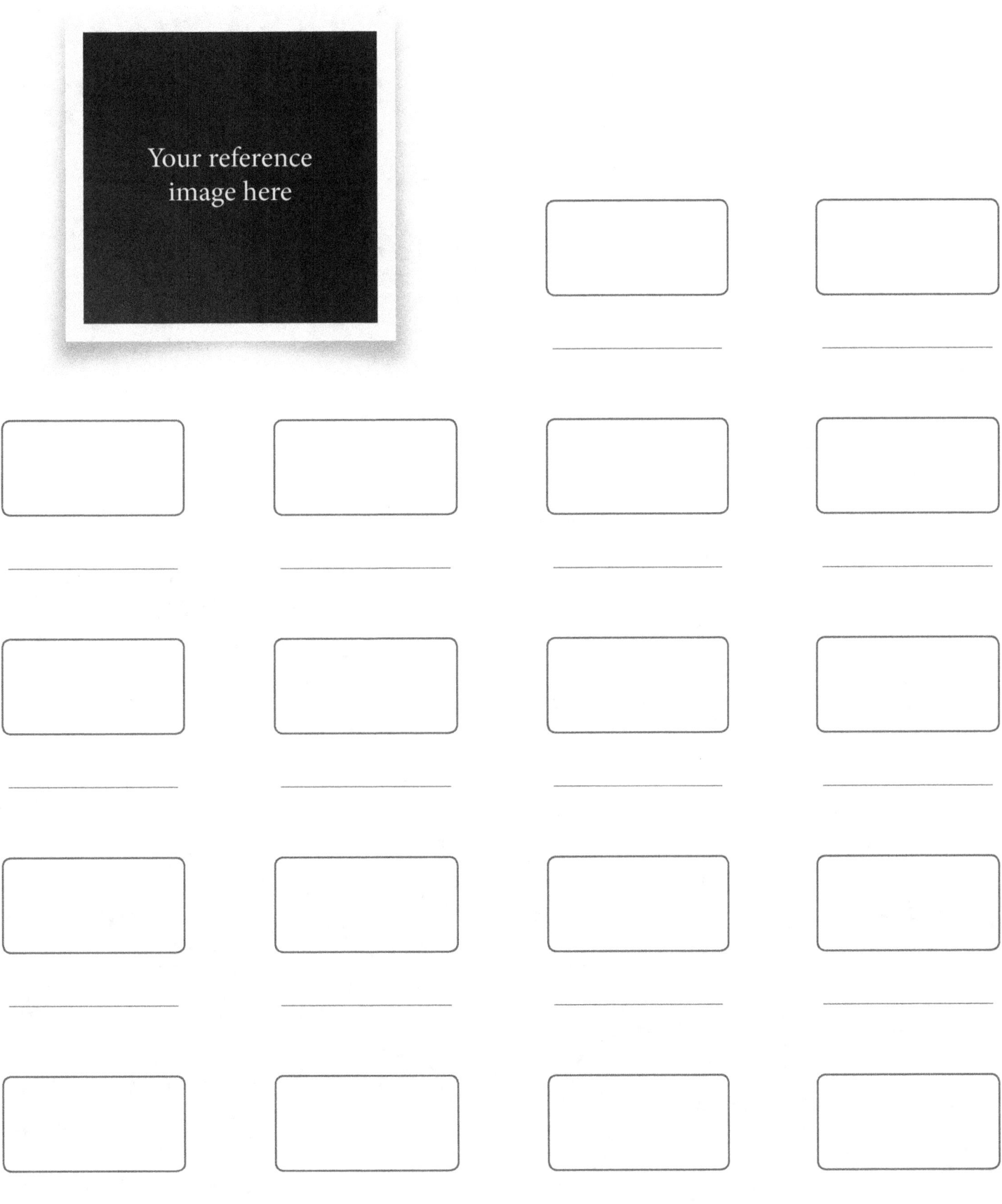

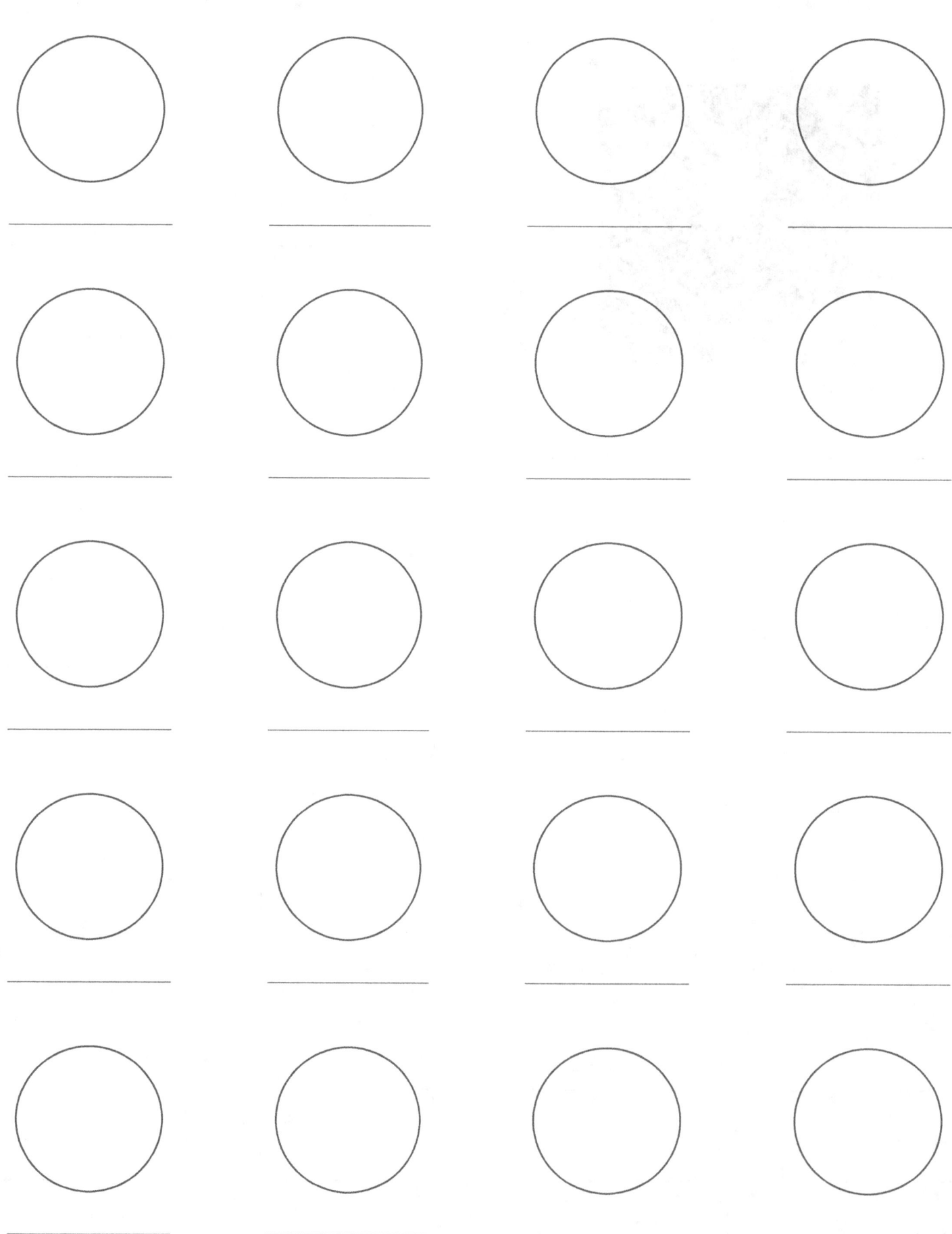

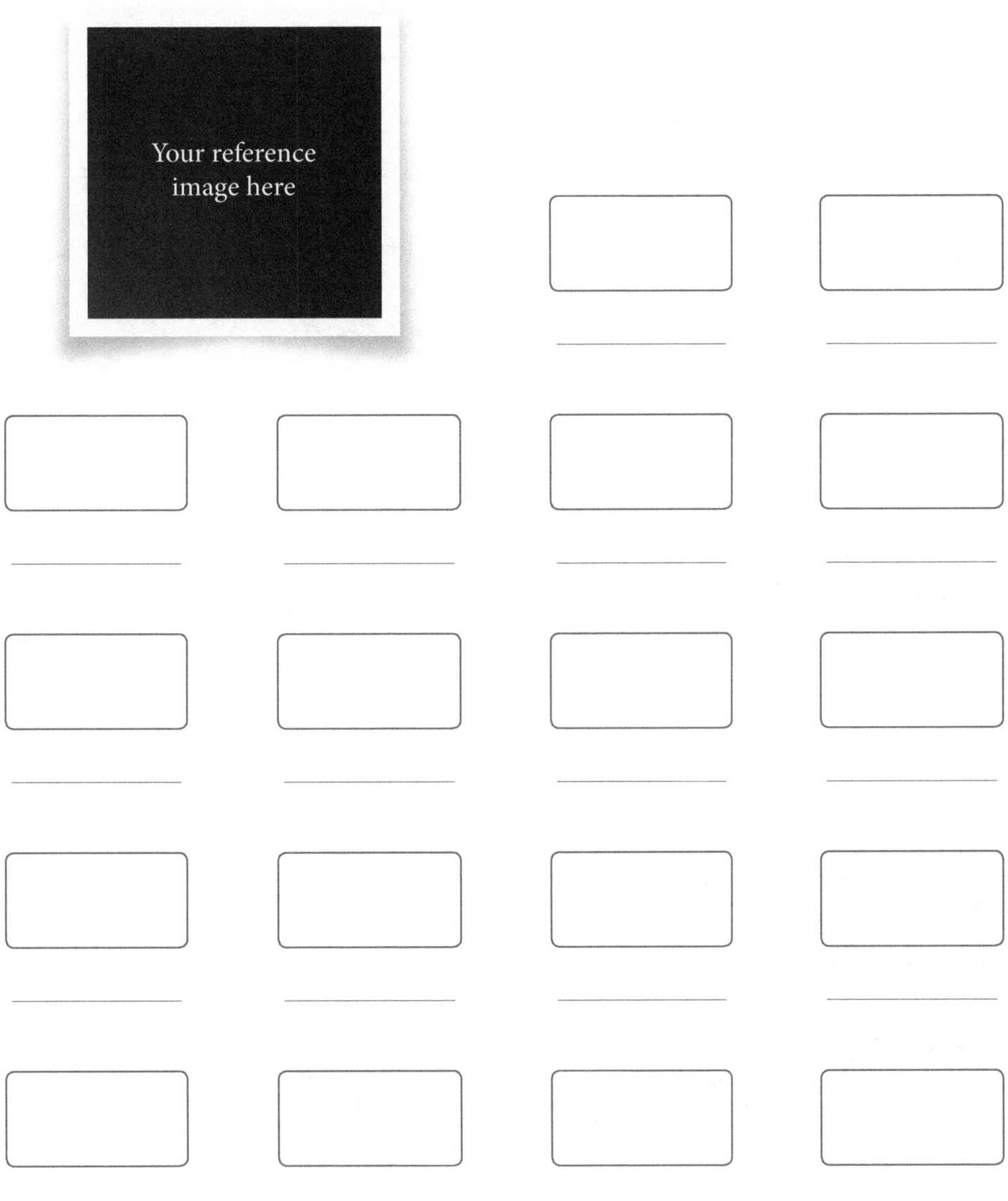

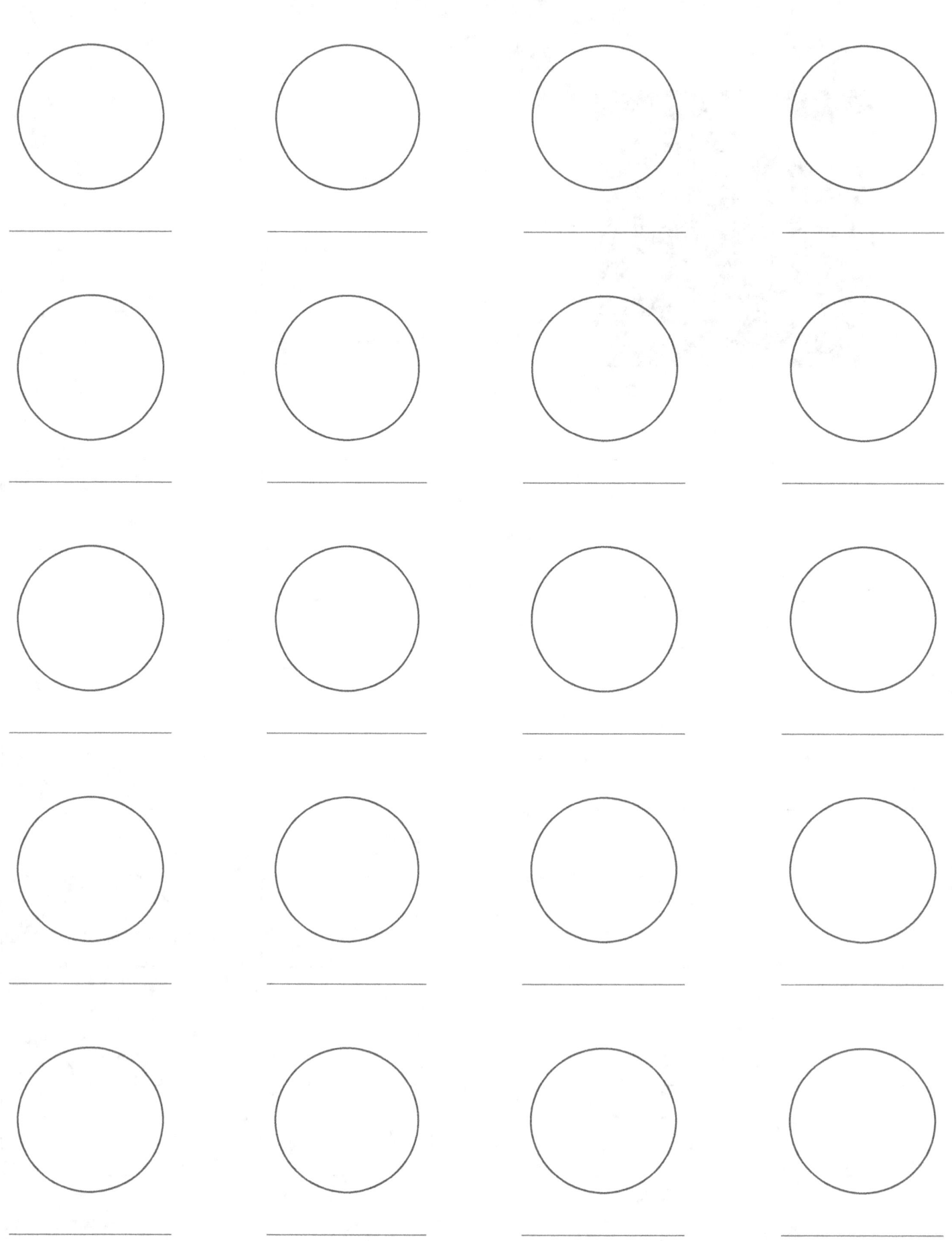

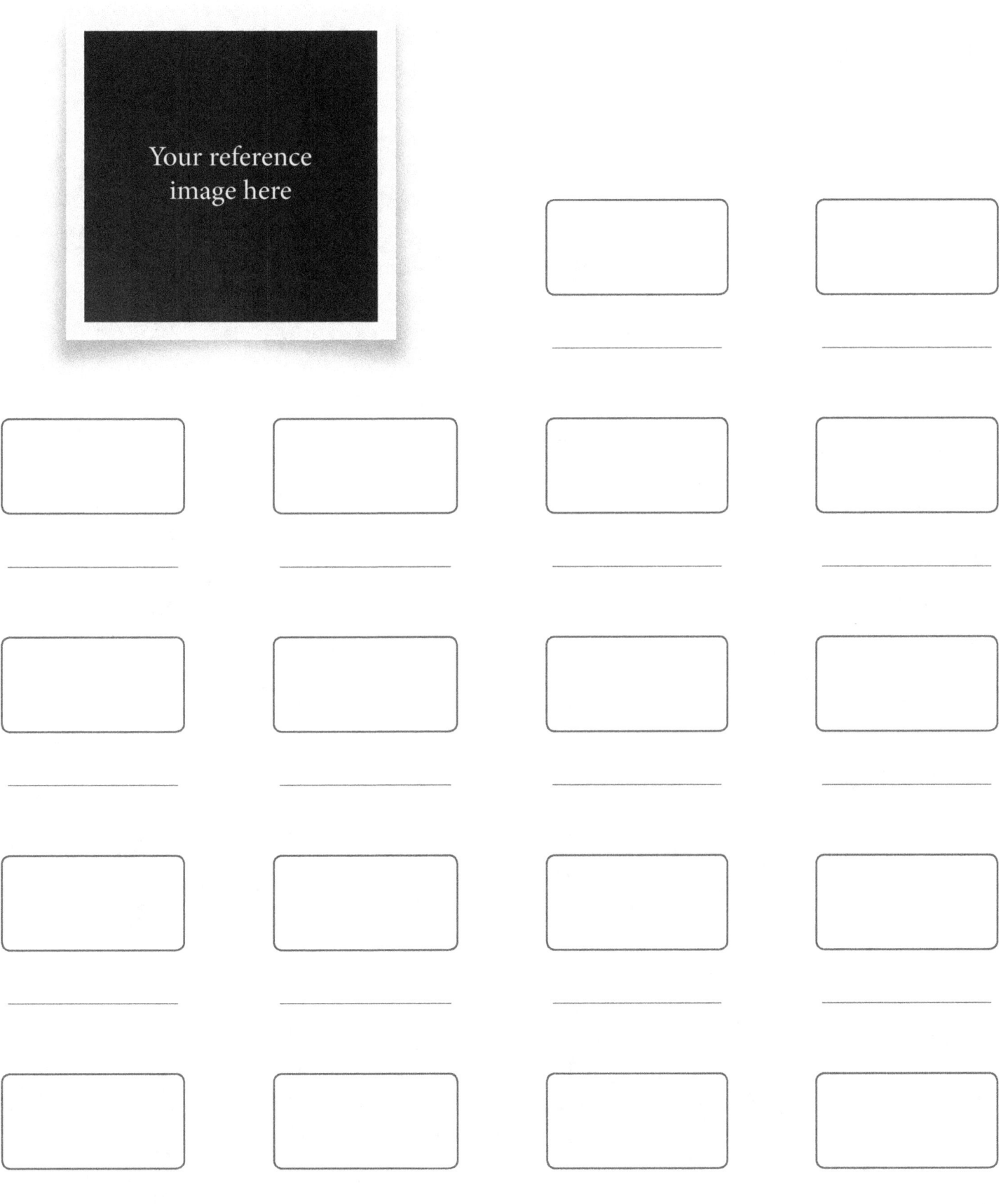

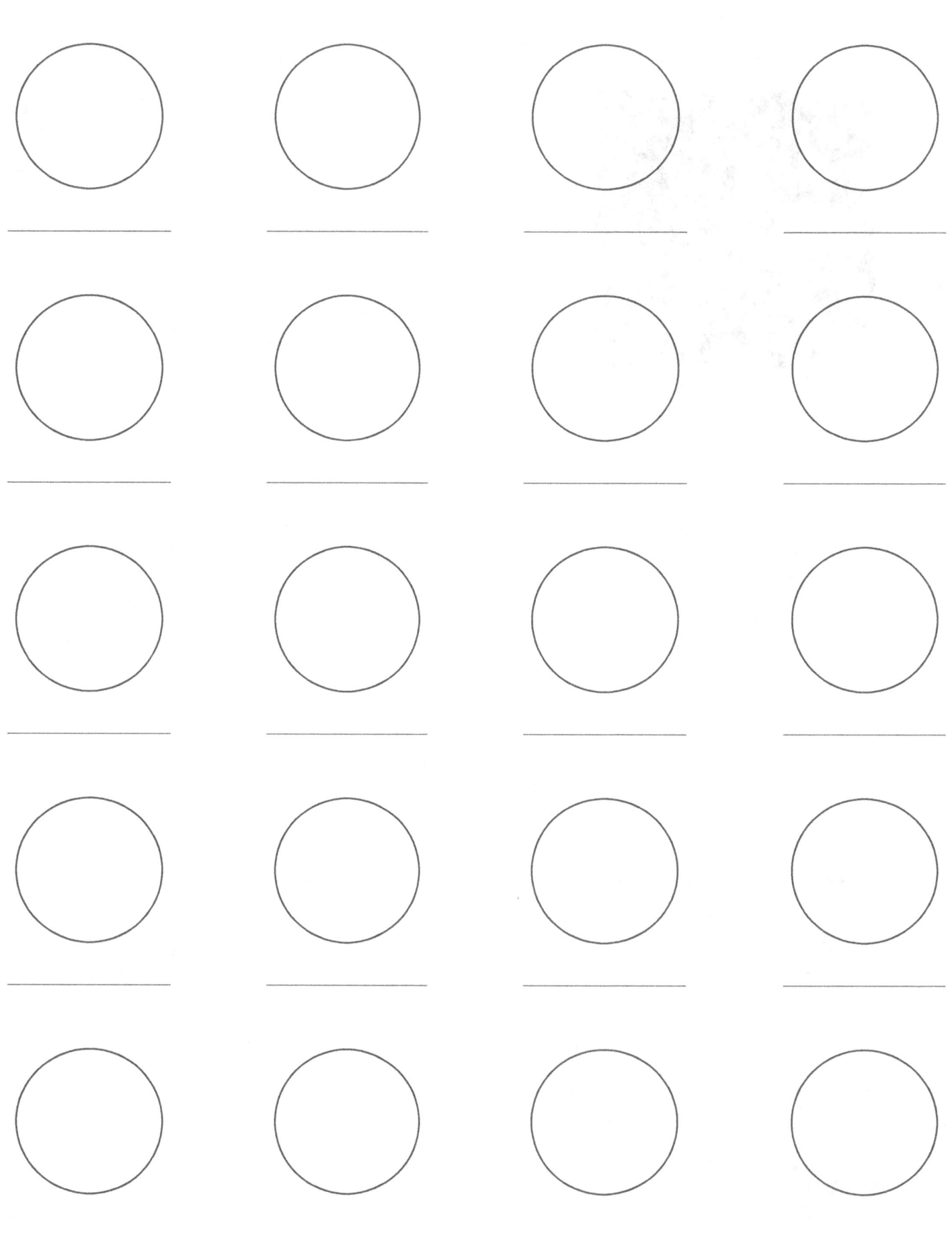

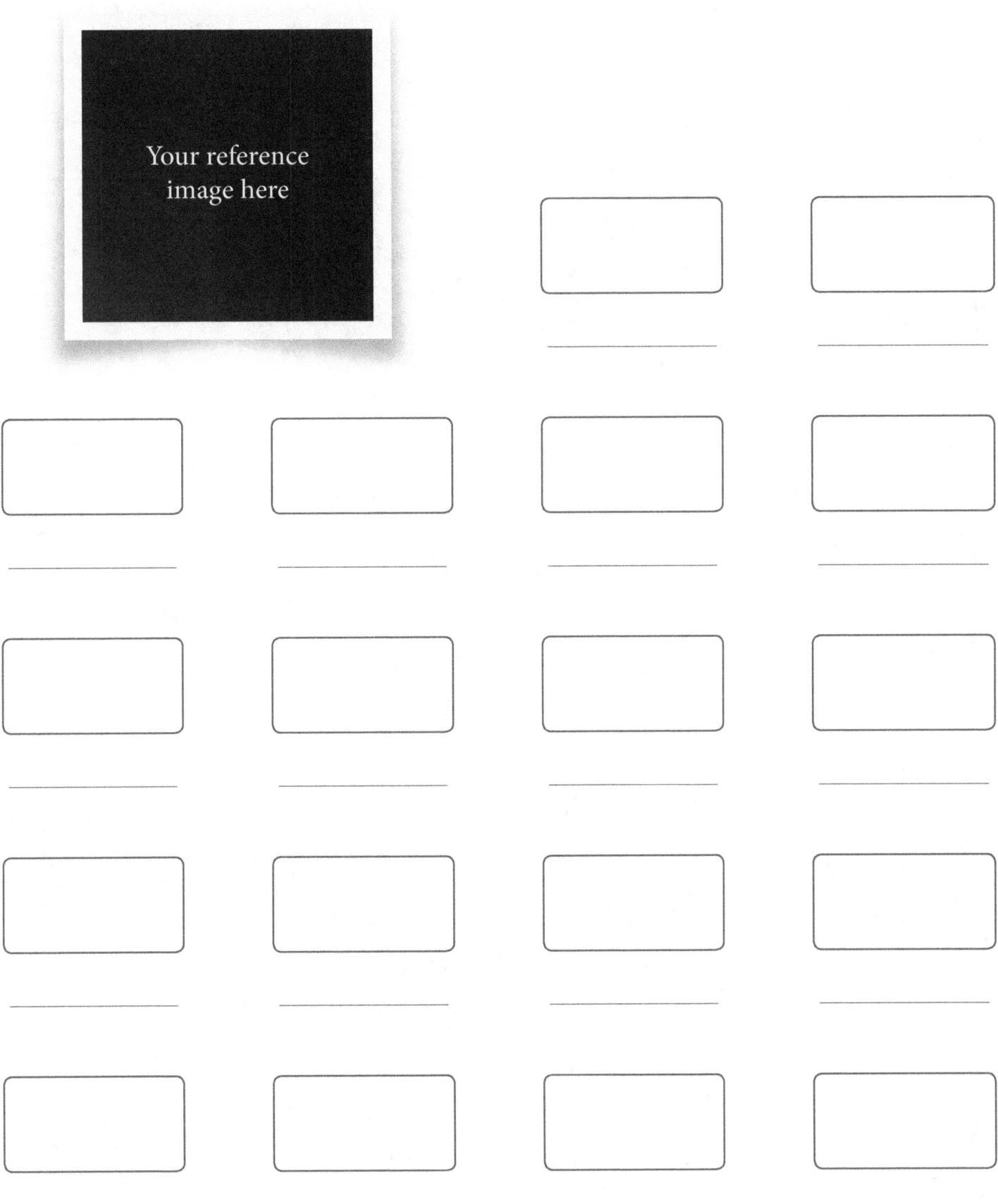

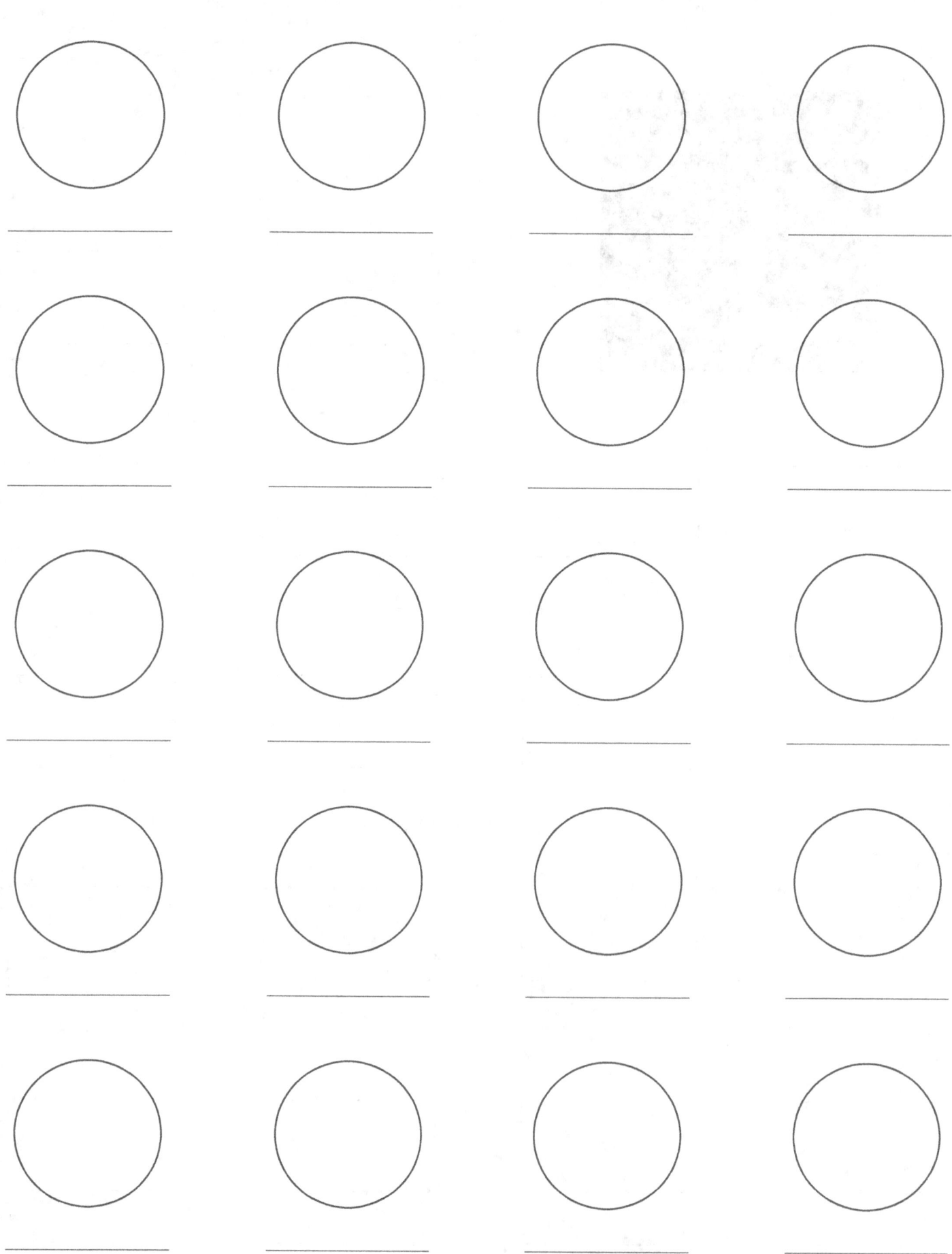

Your reference image here

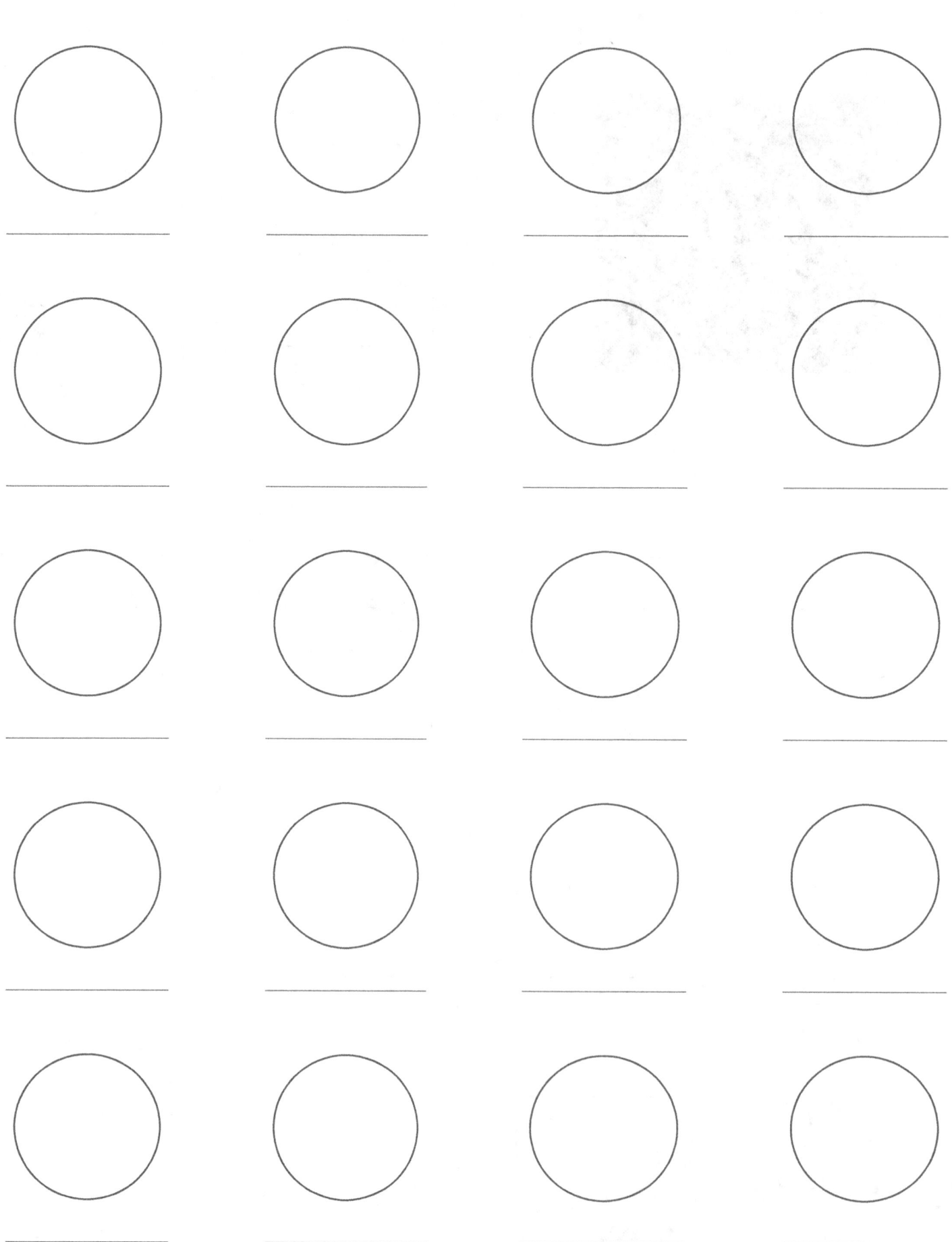

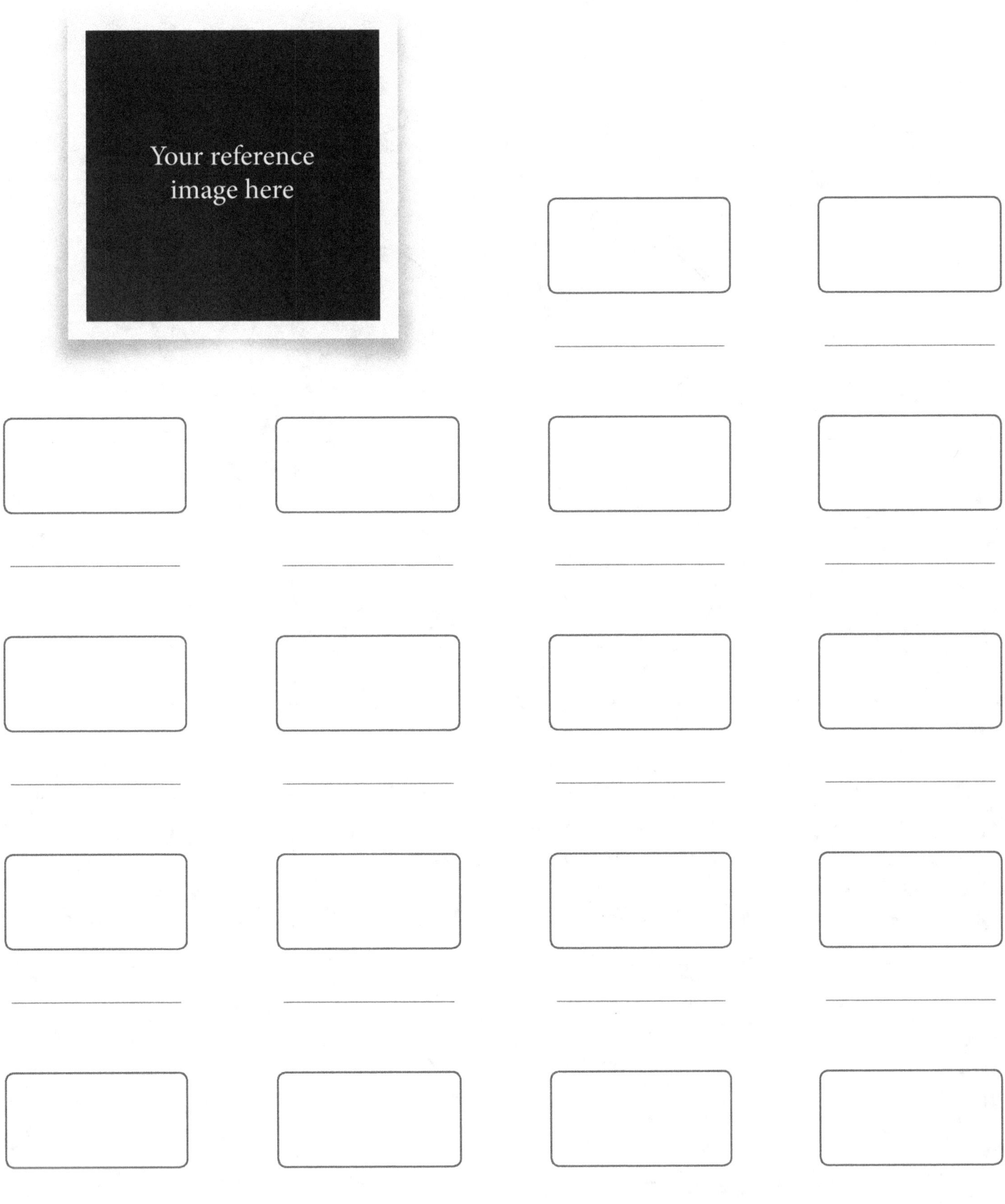

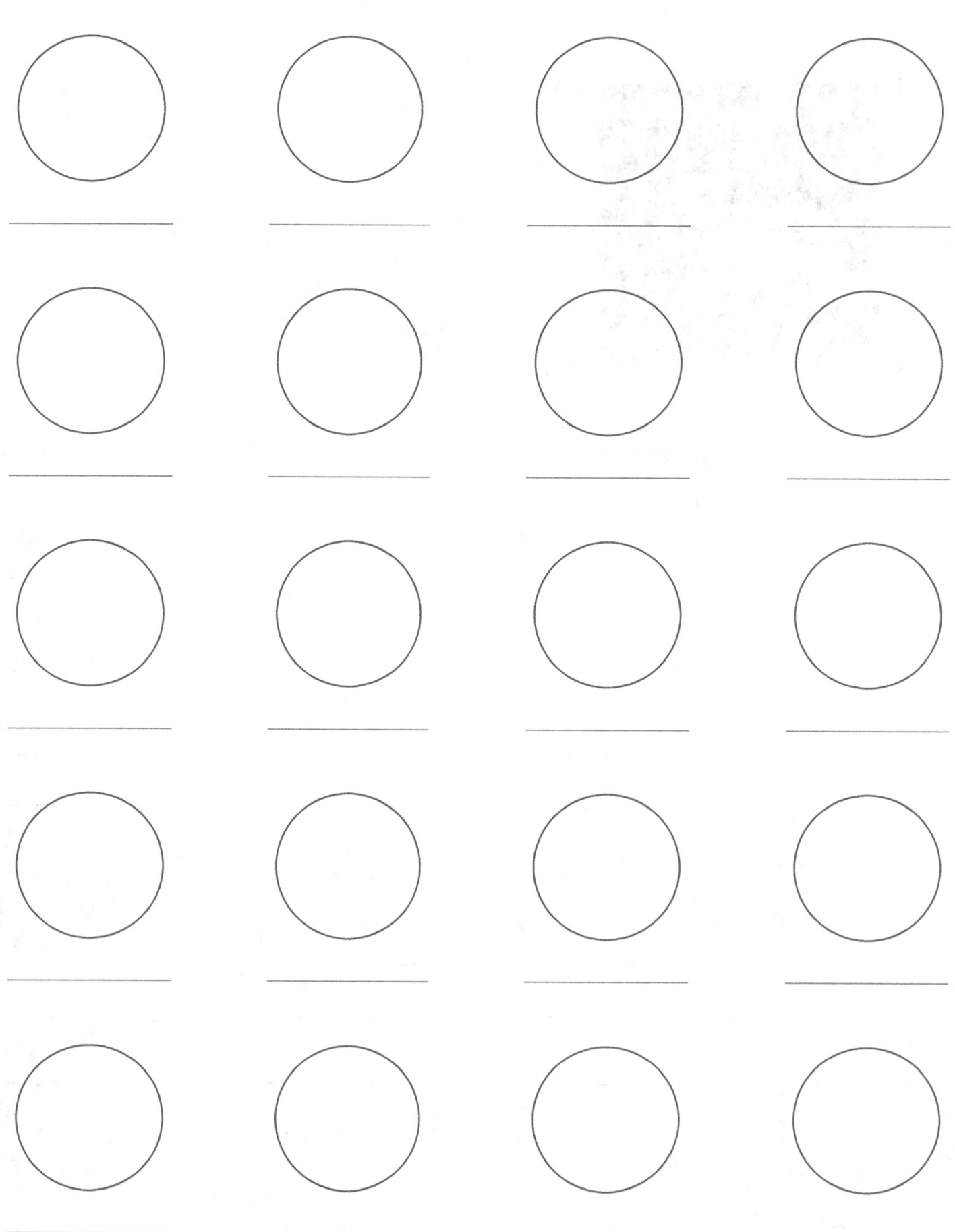

Your reference image here

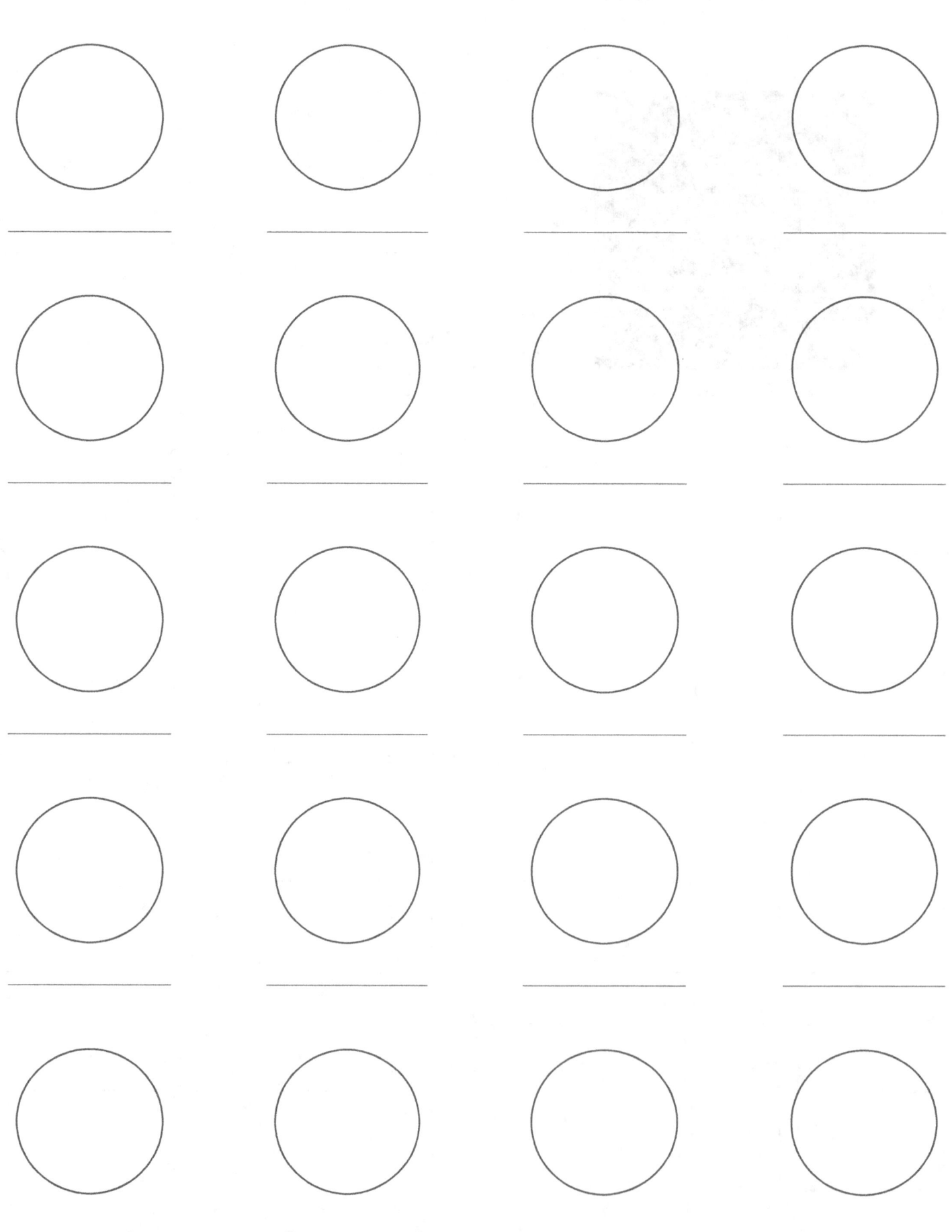

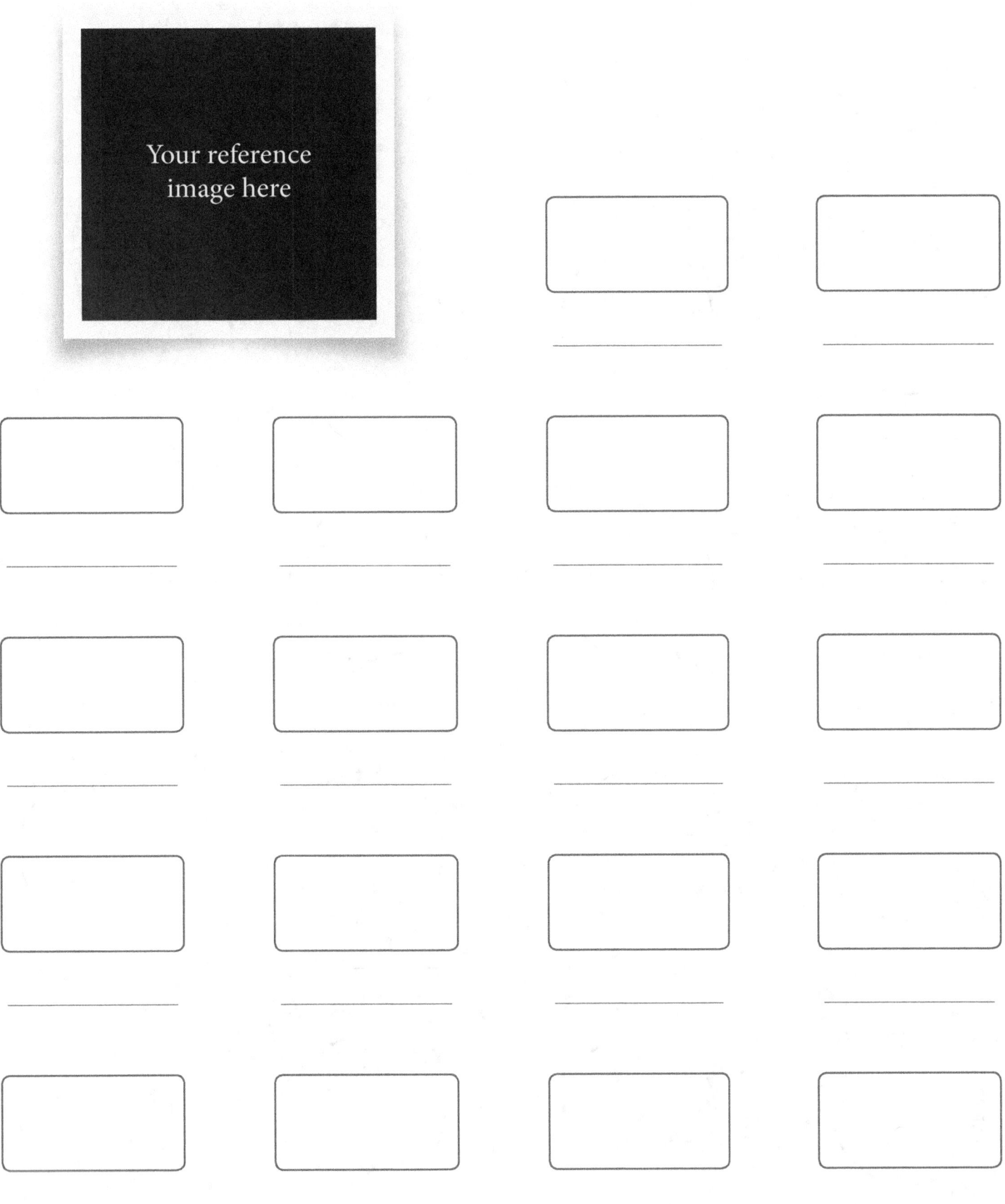

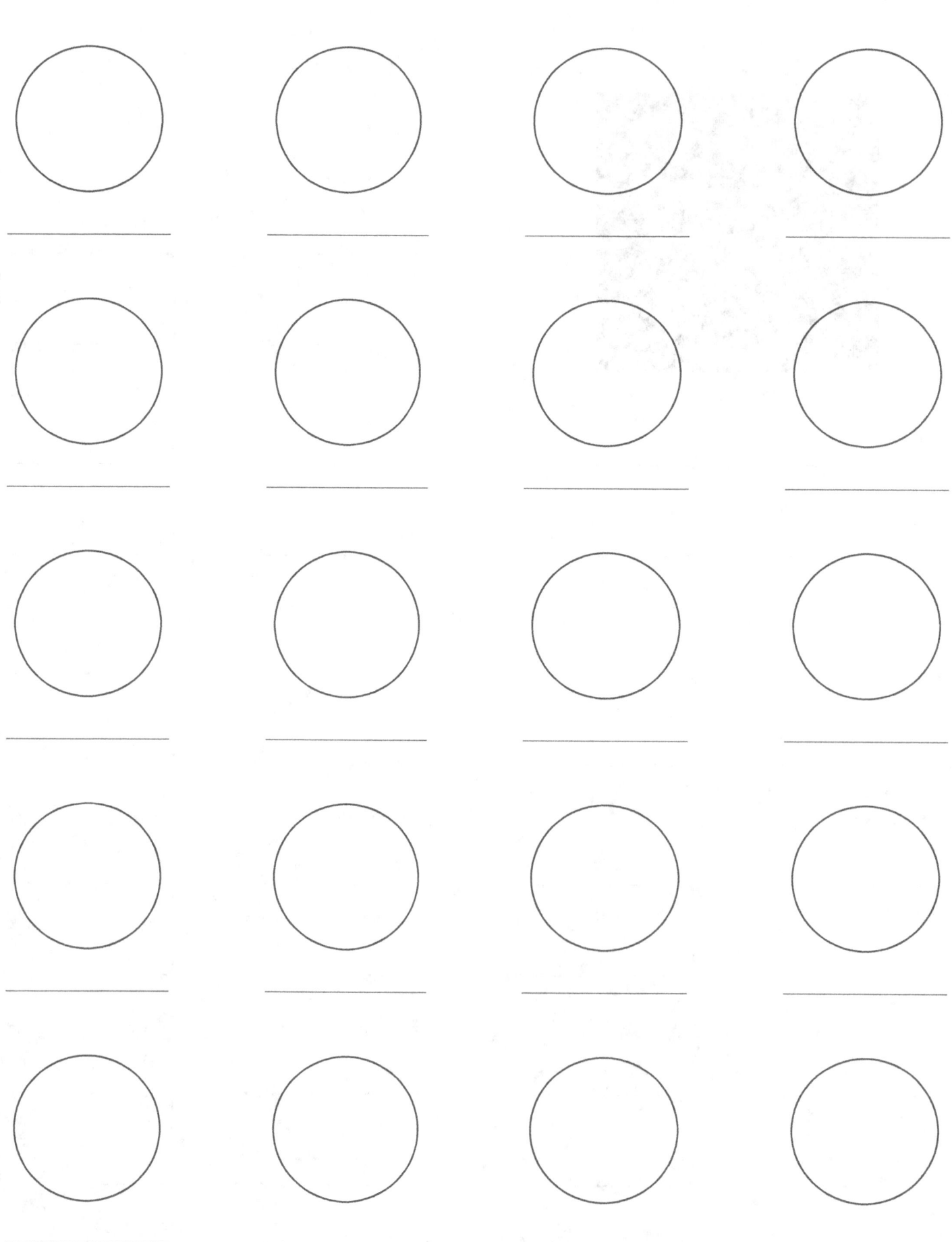

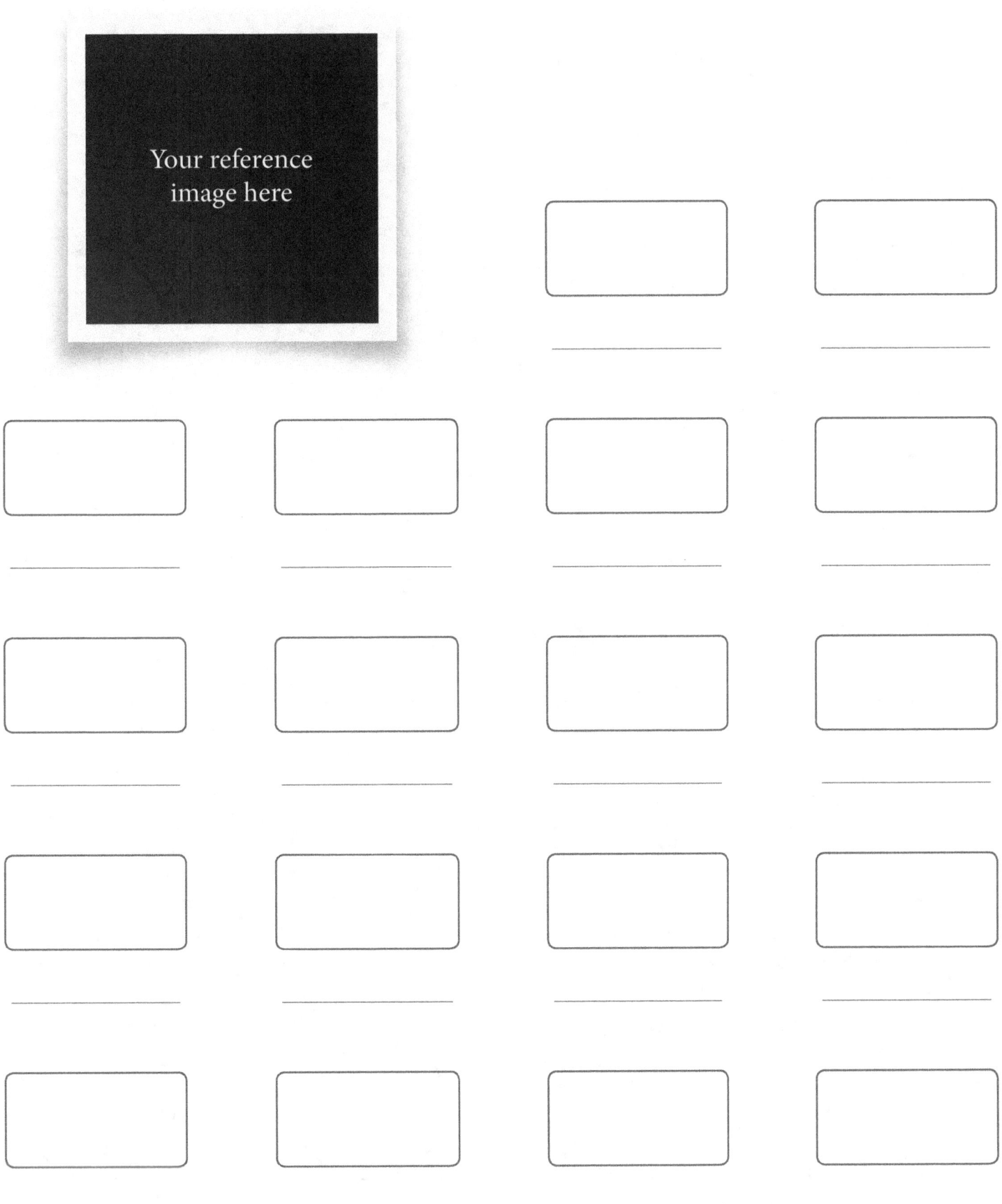

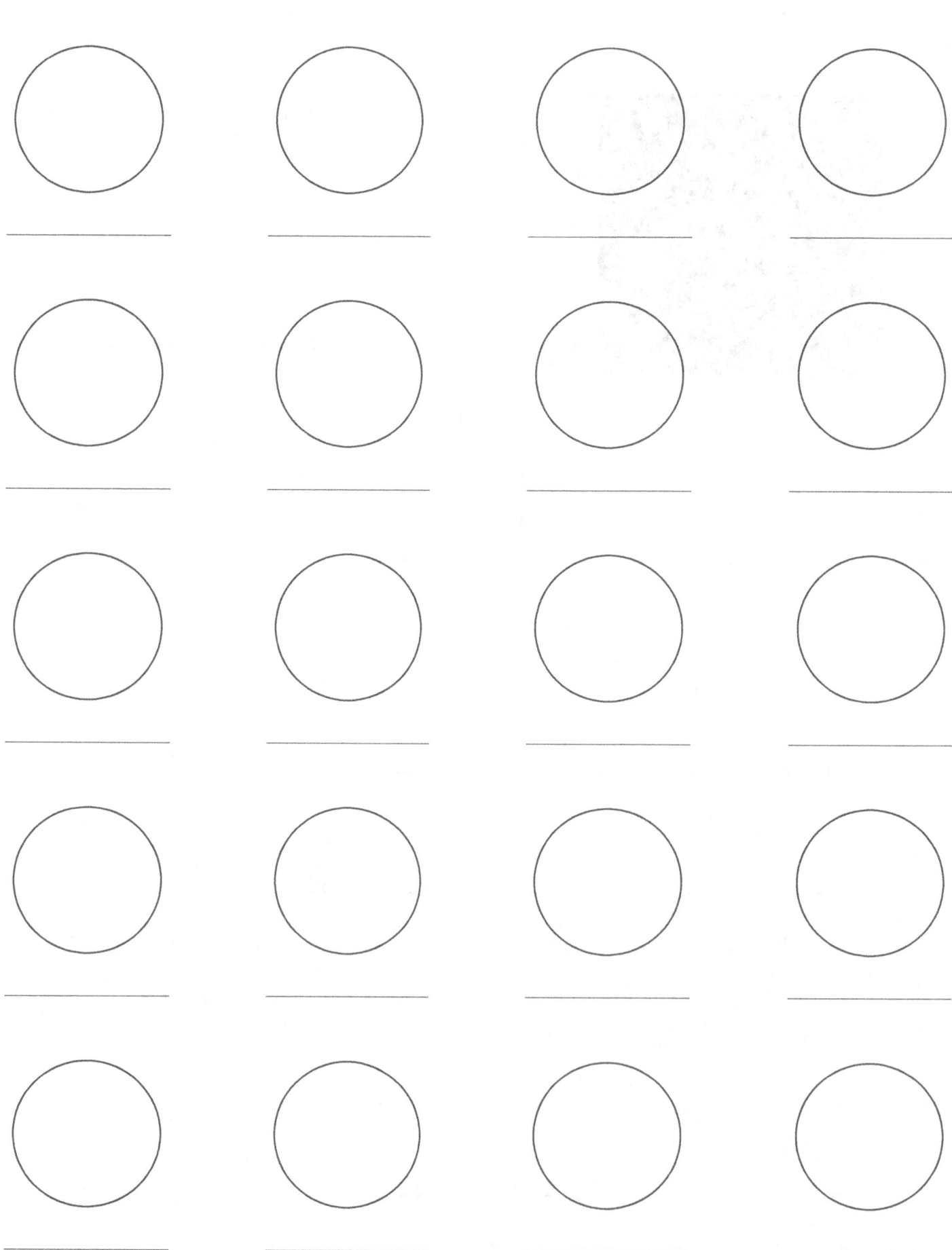

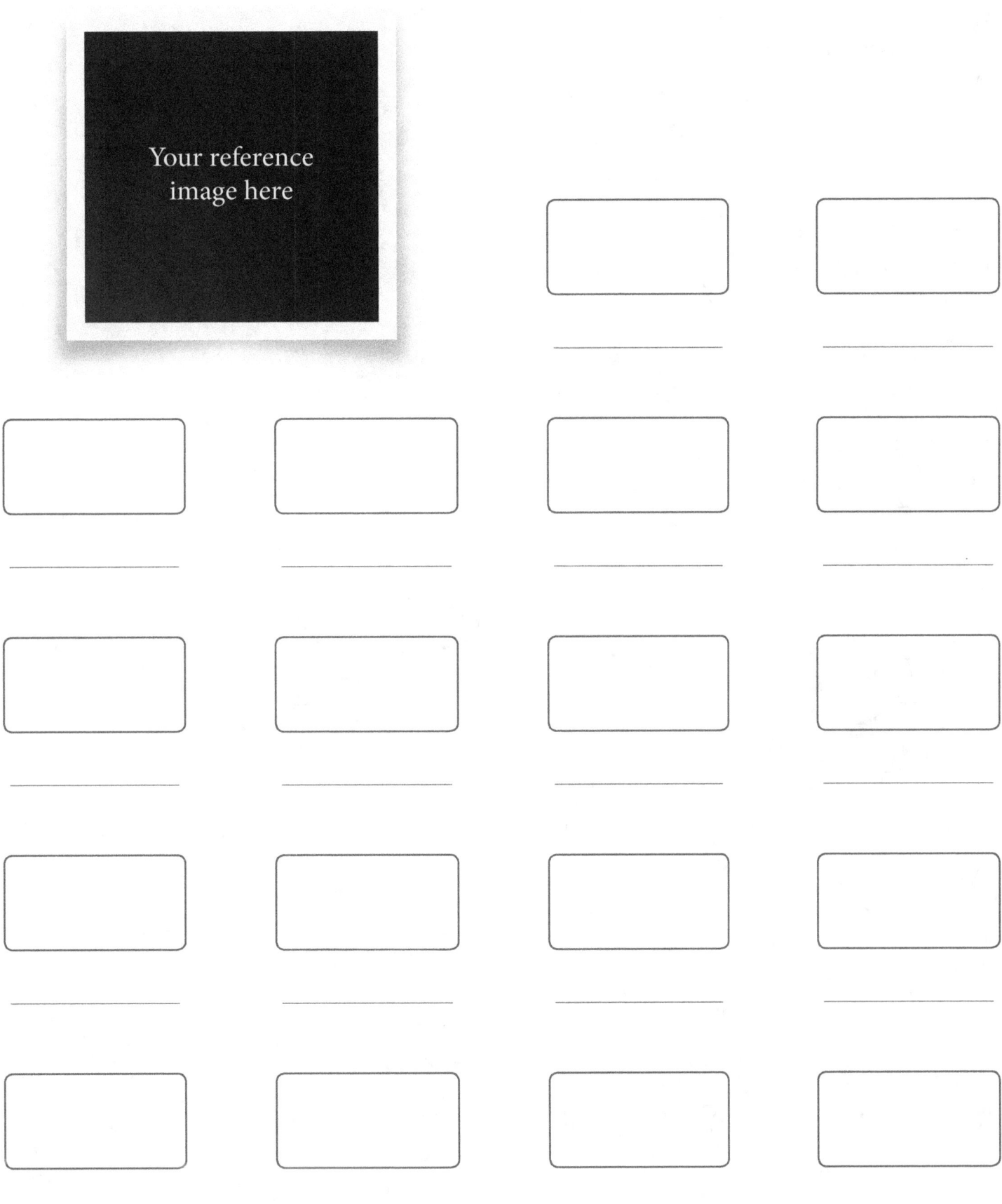

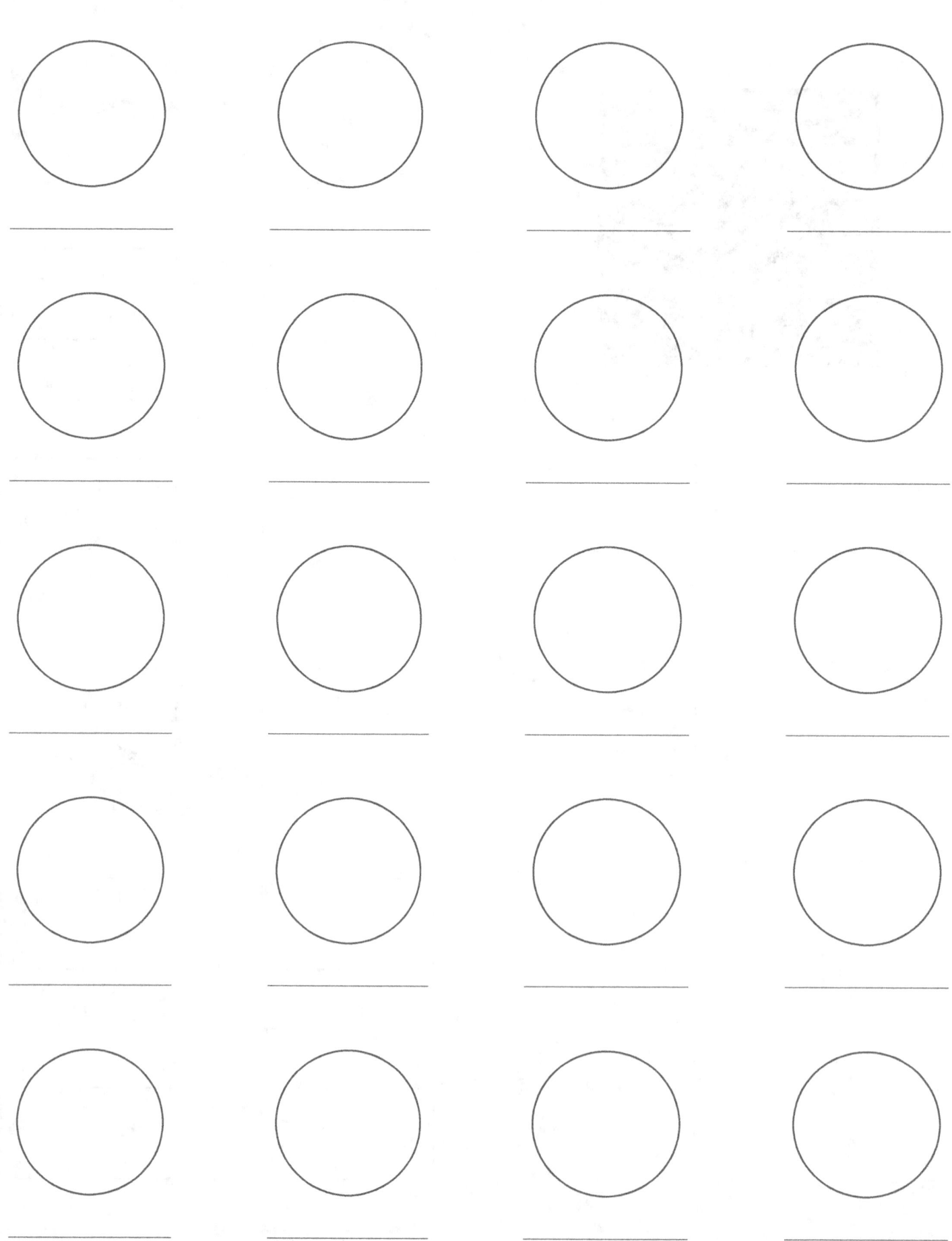

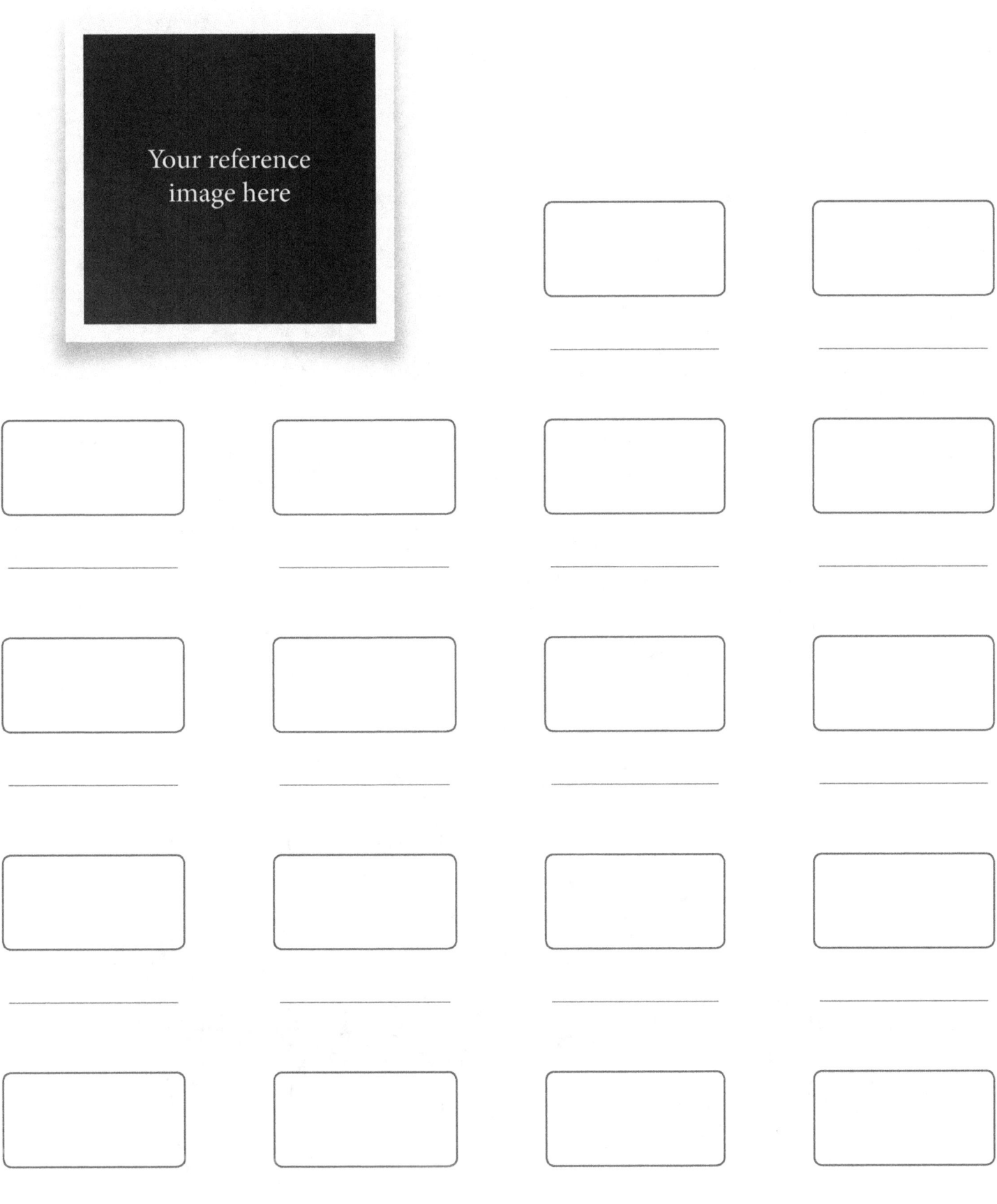

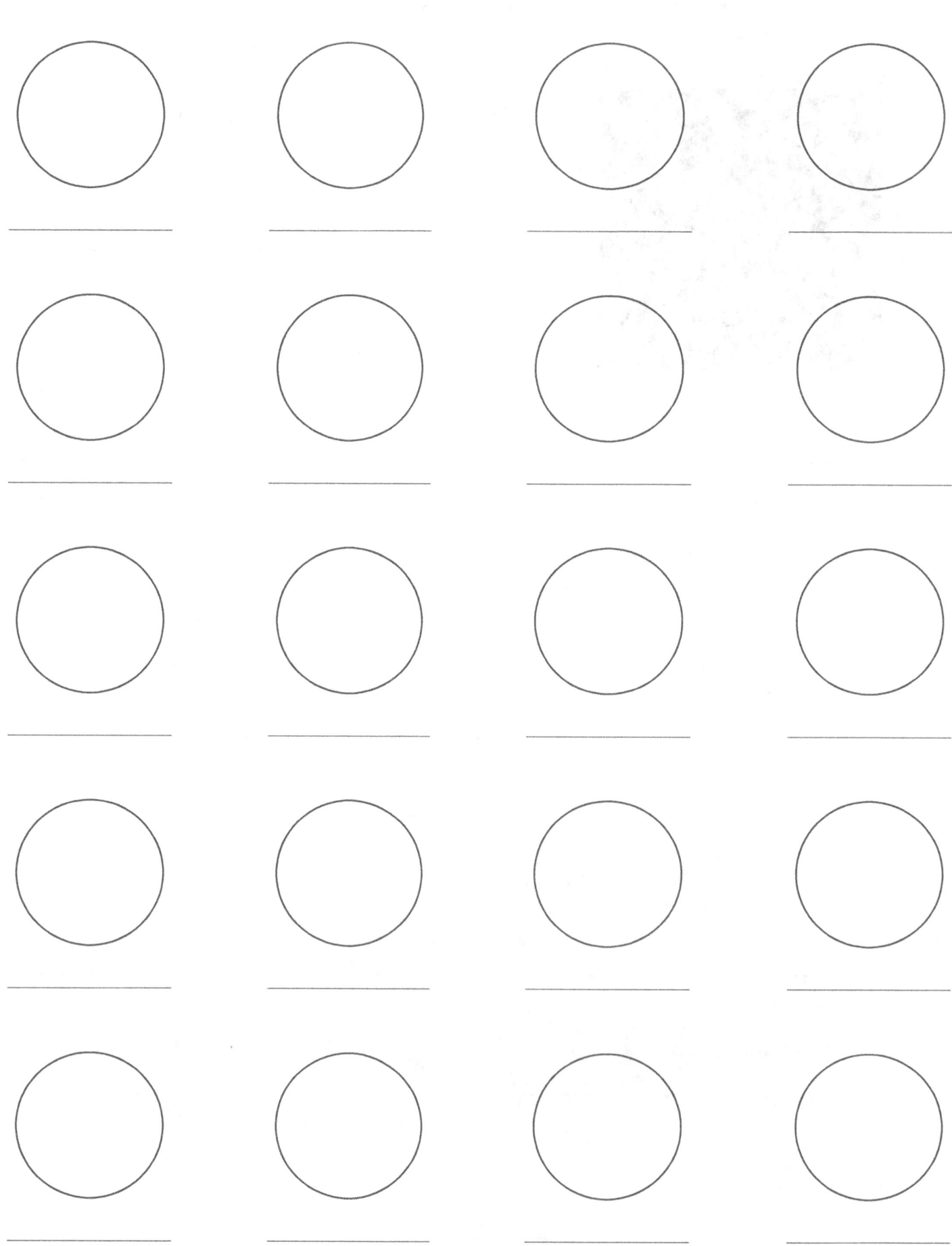

Your reference image here

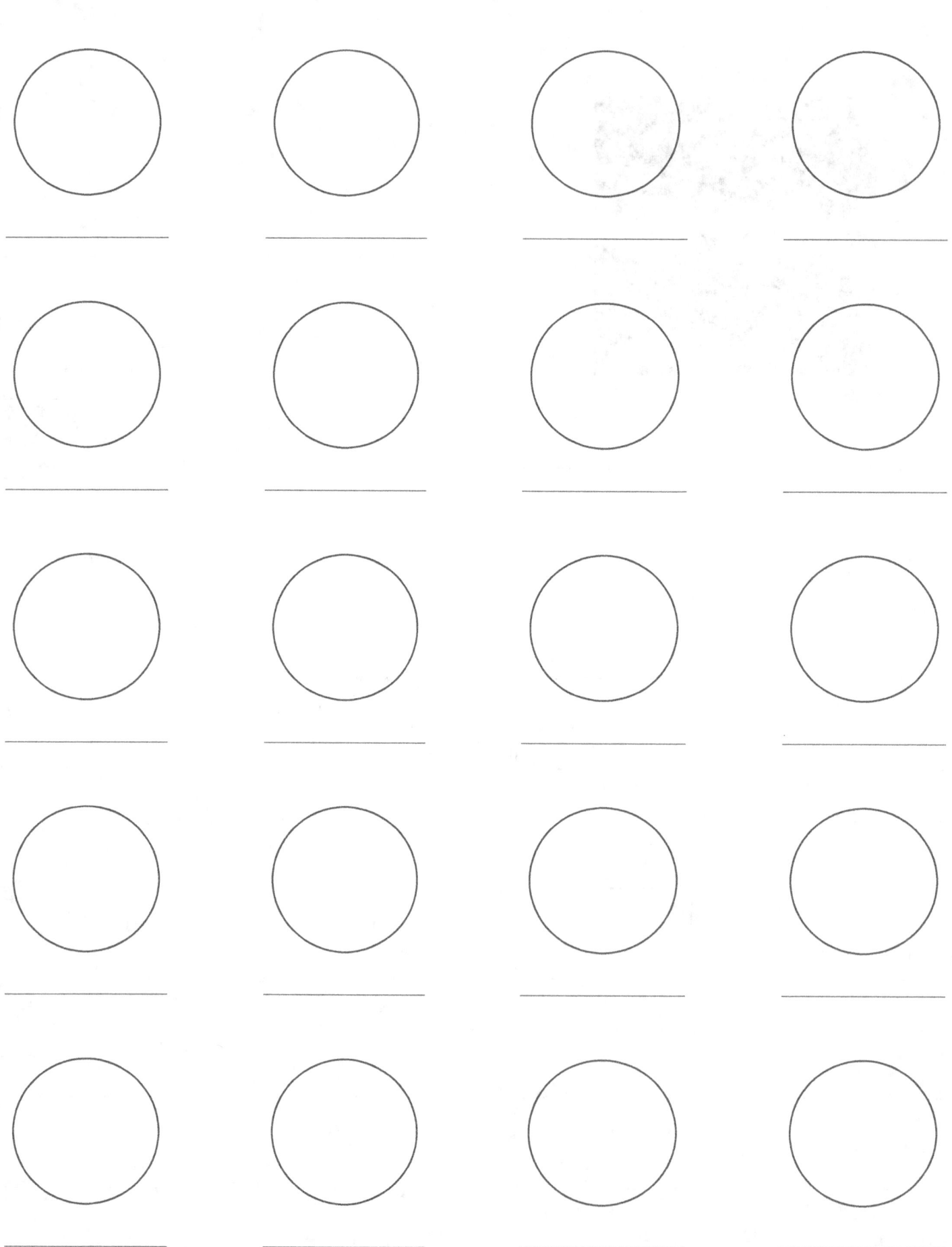

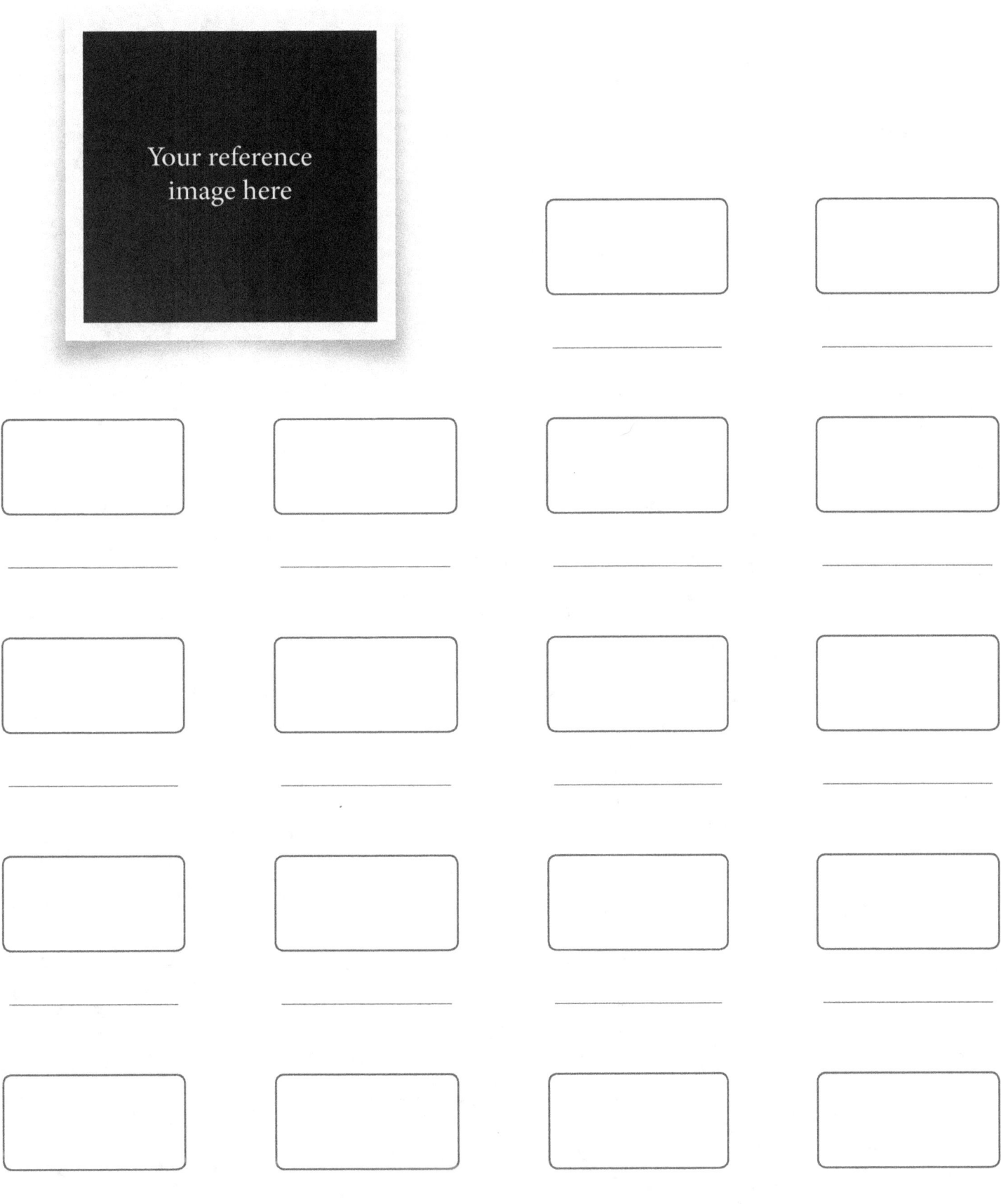

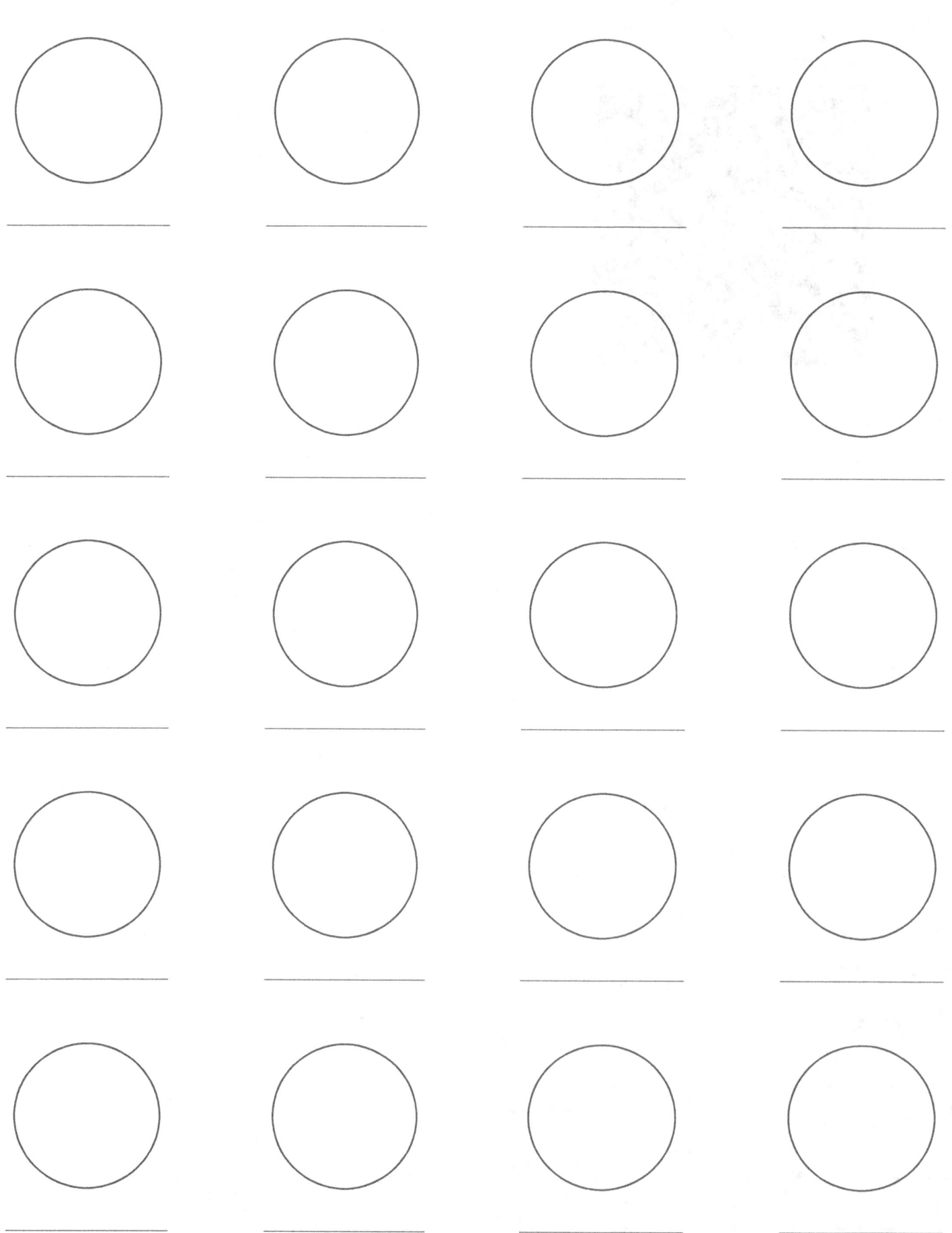

Your reference image here

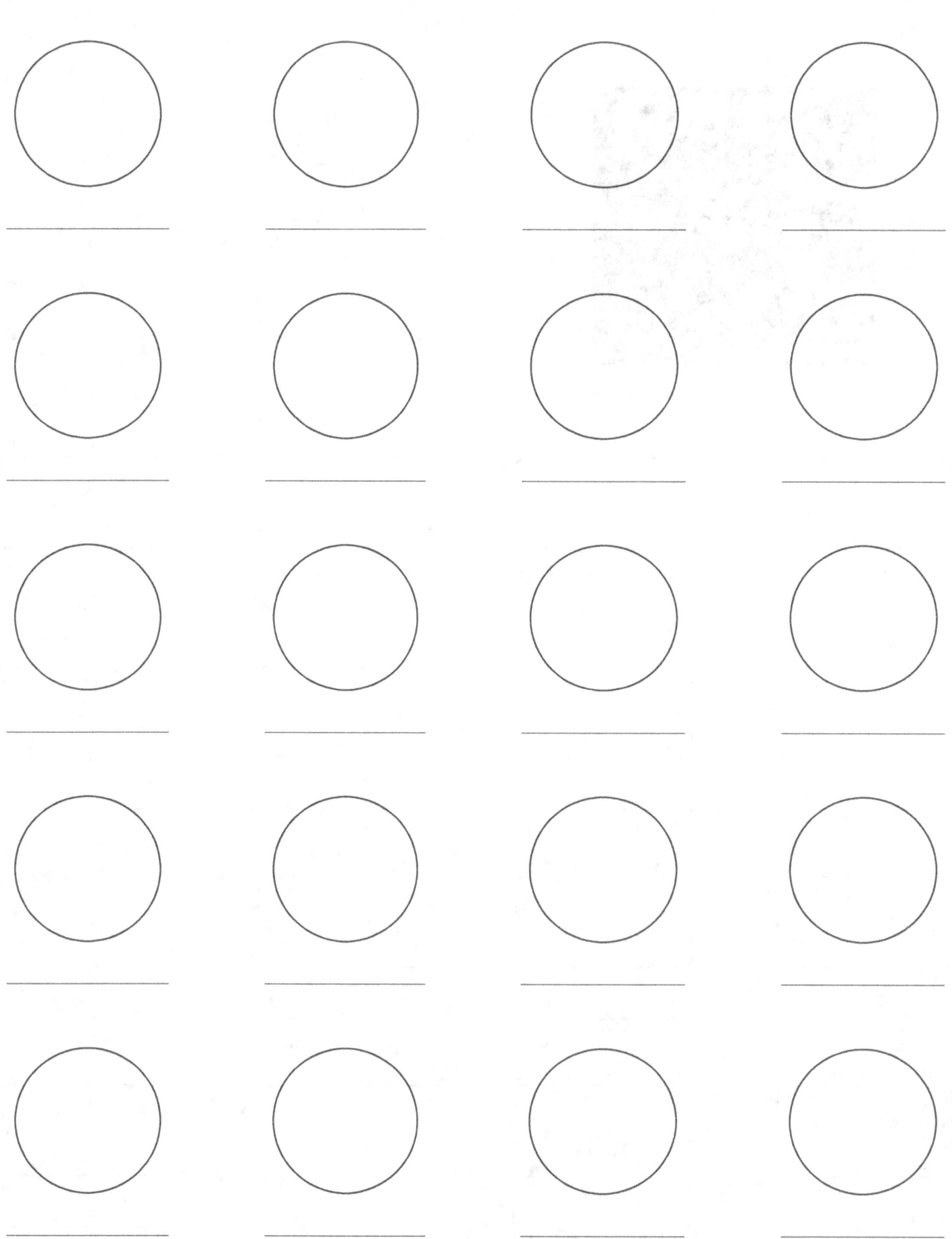

Your reference image here

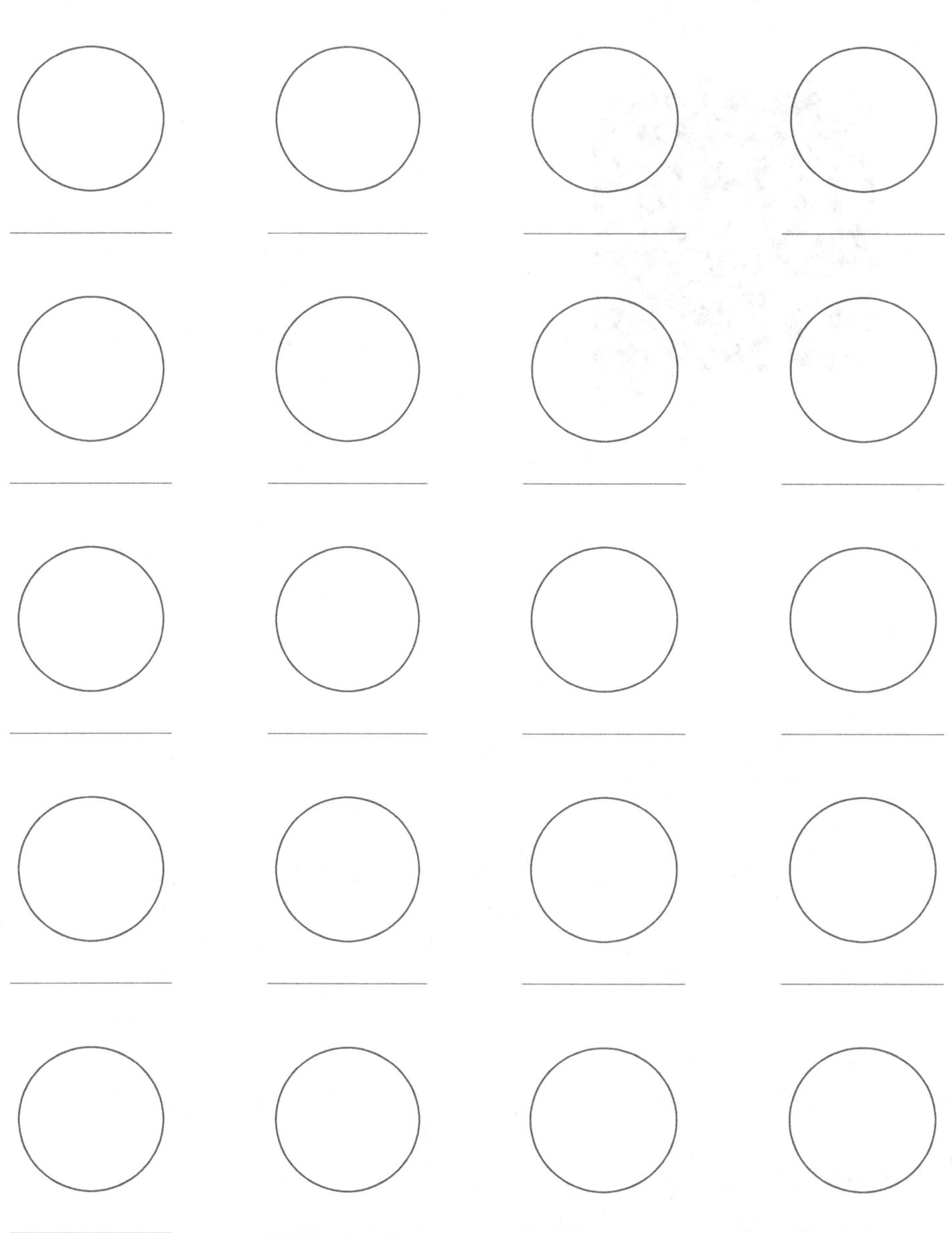

Your reference image here

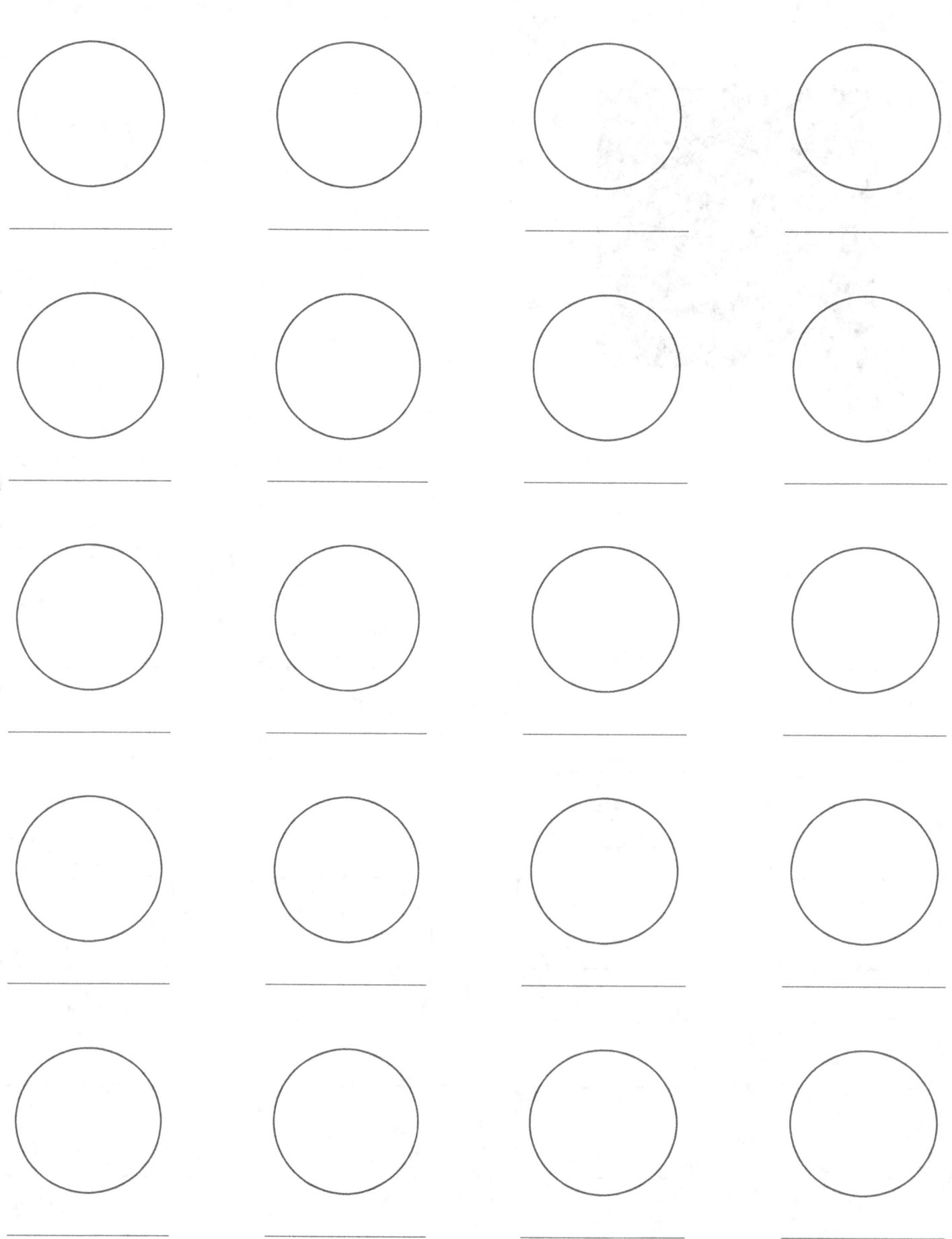

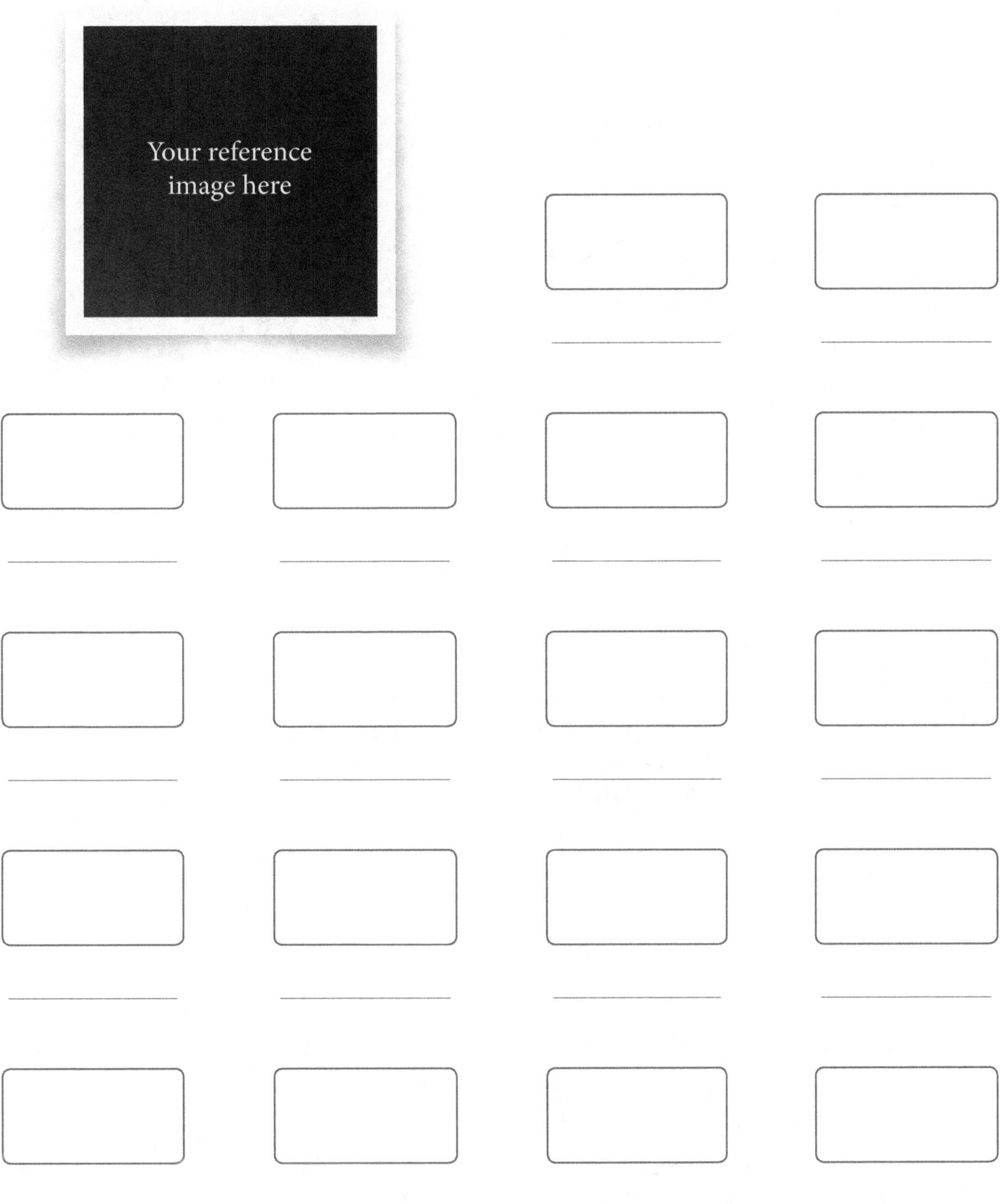

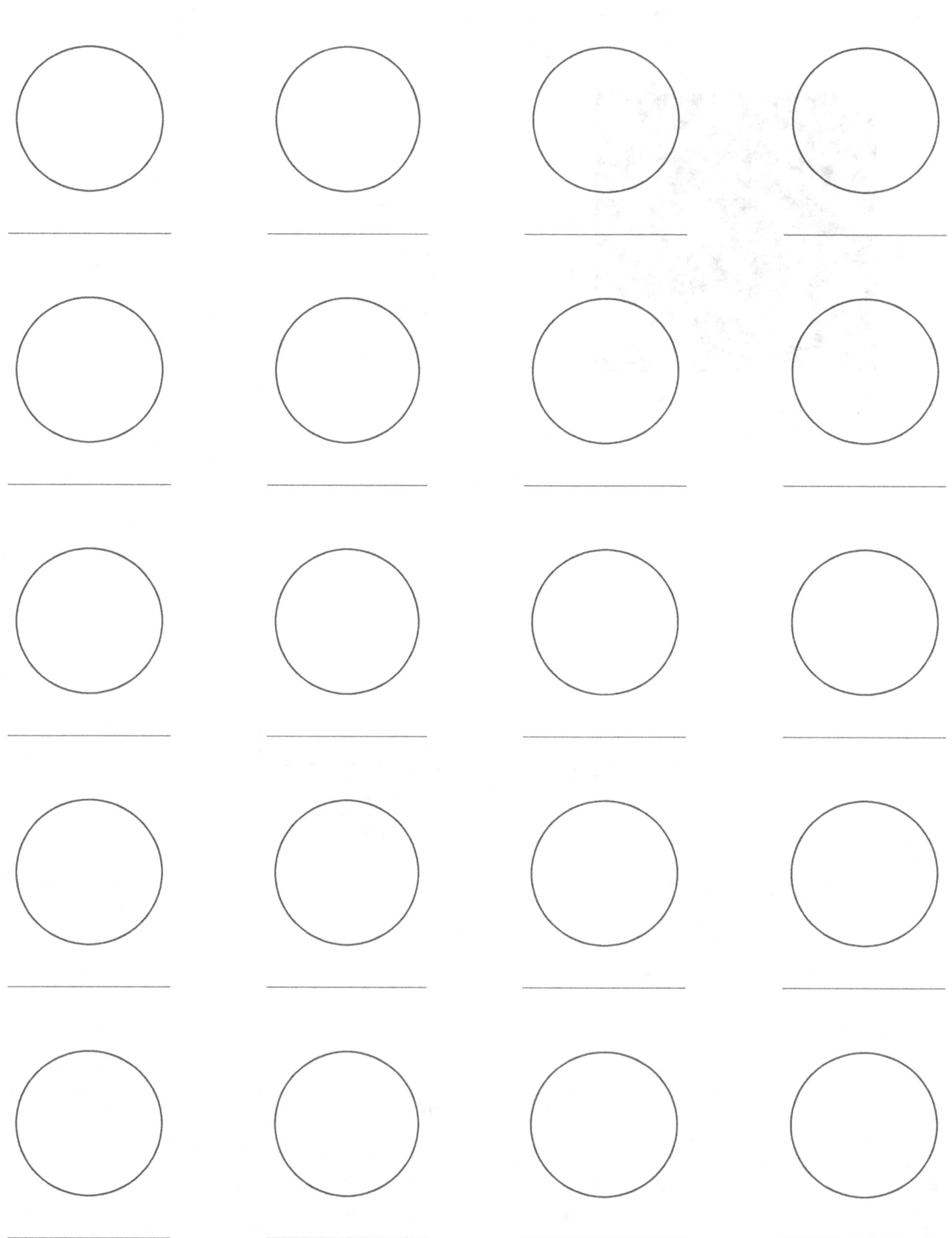

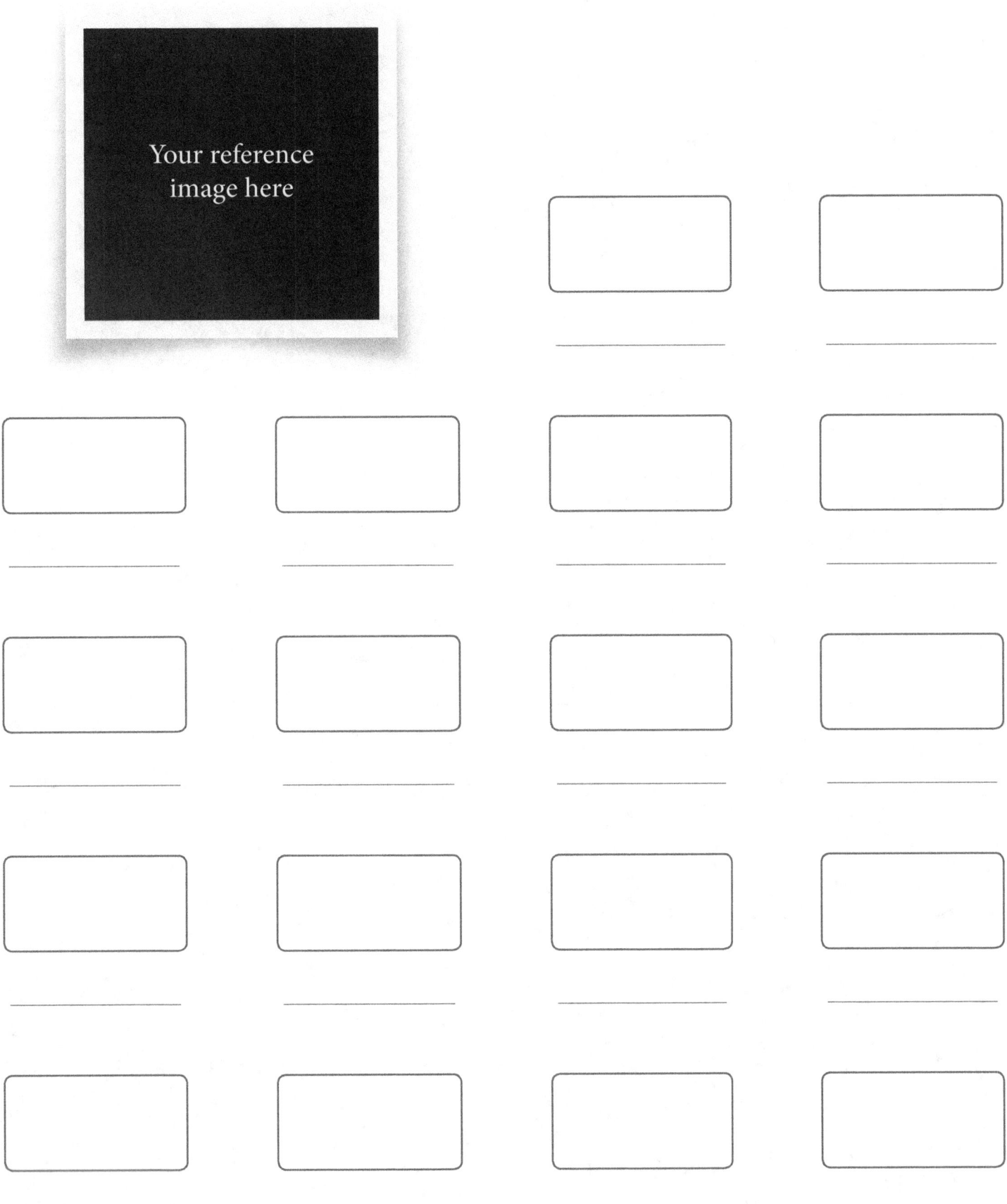

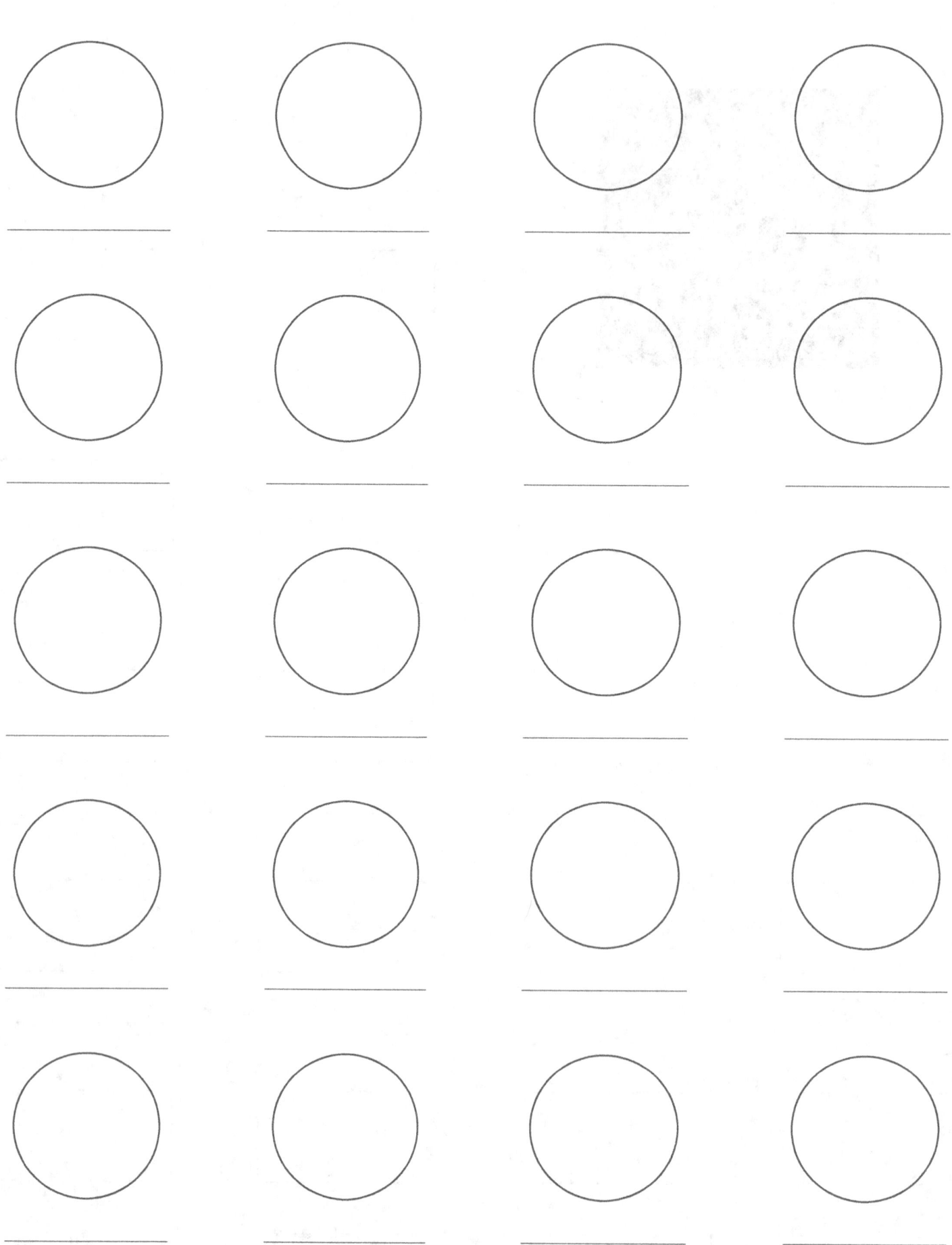

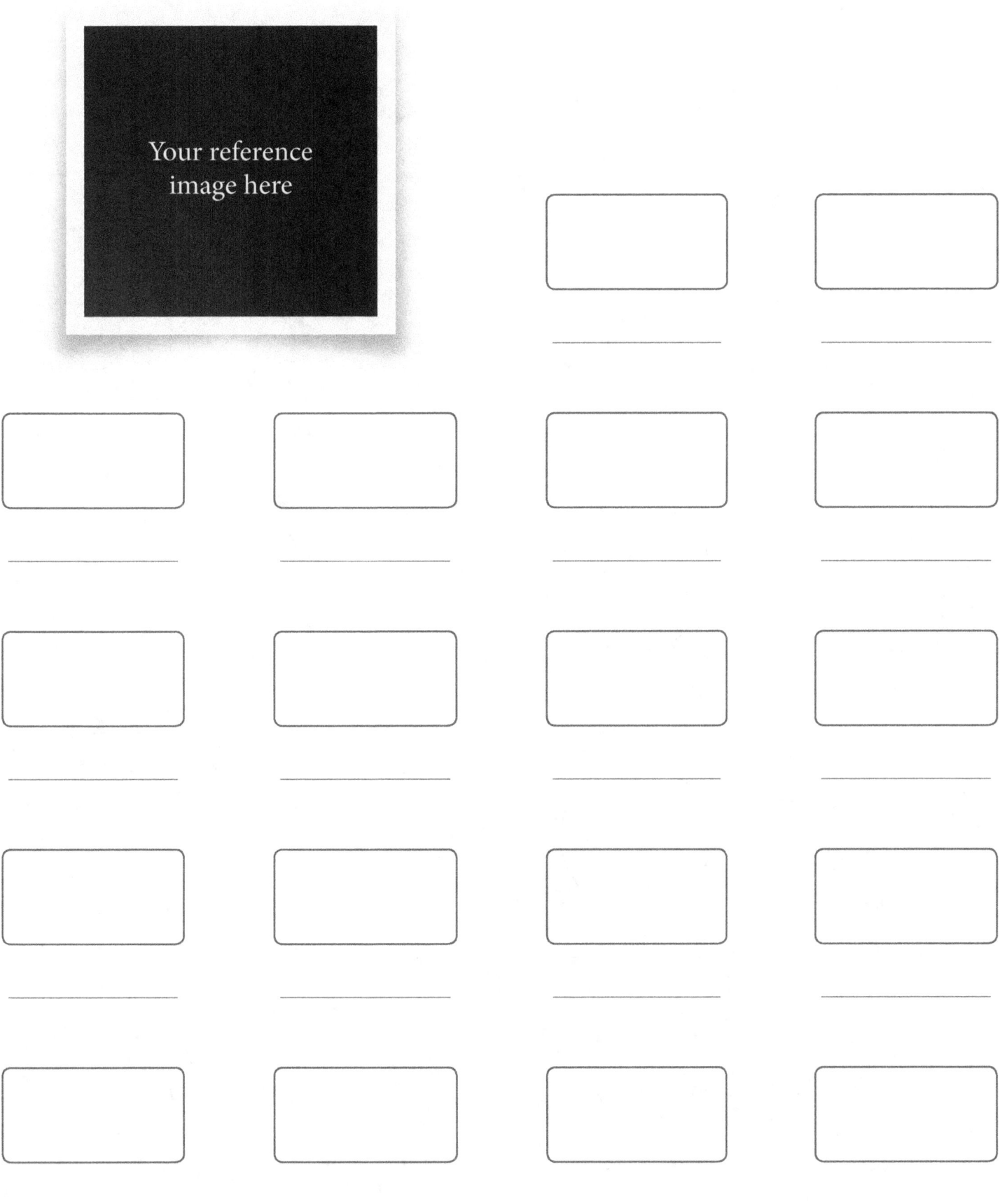

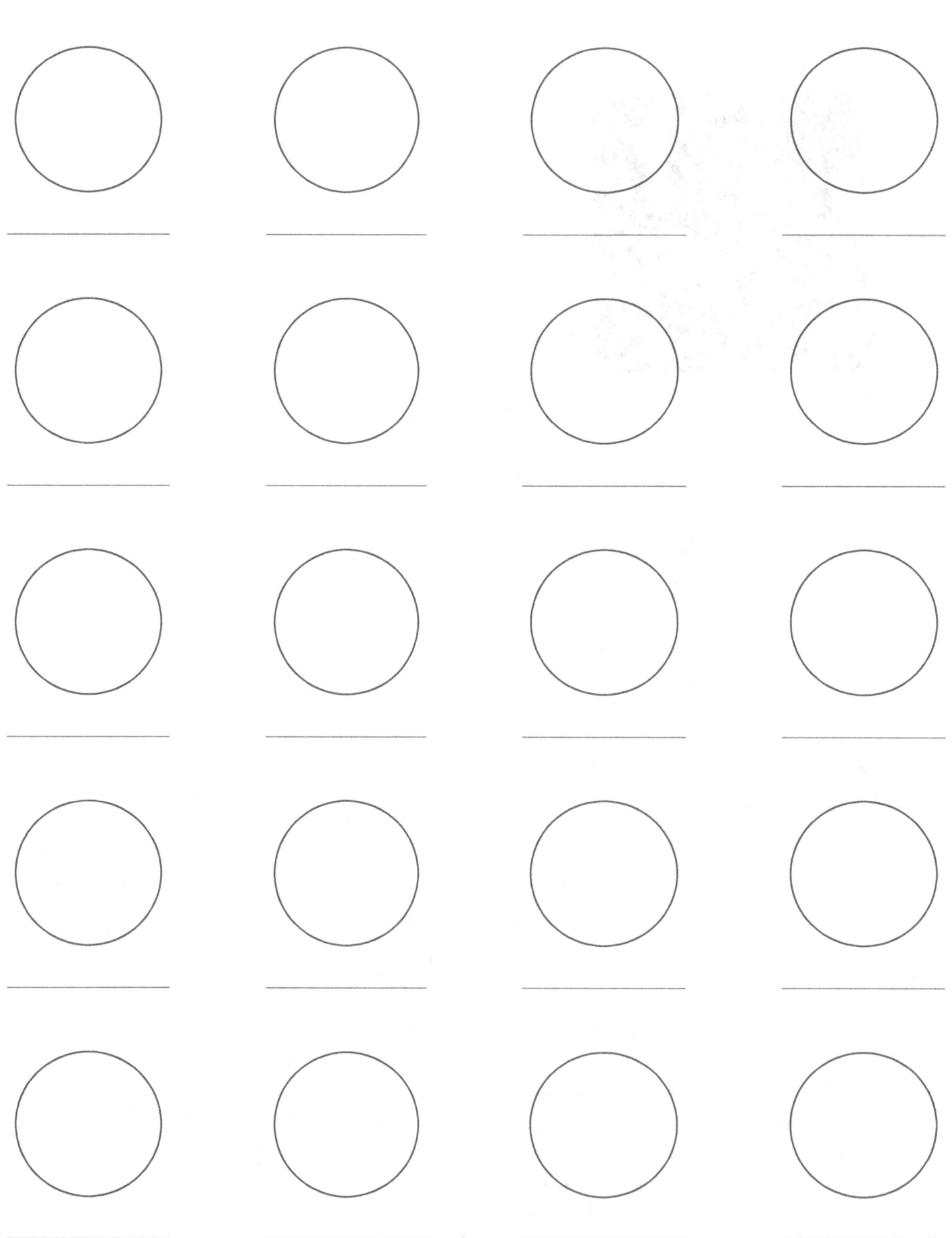

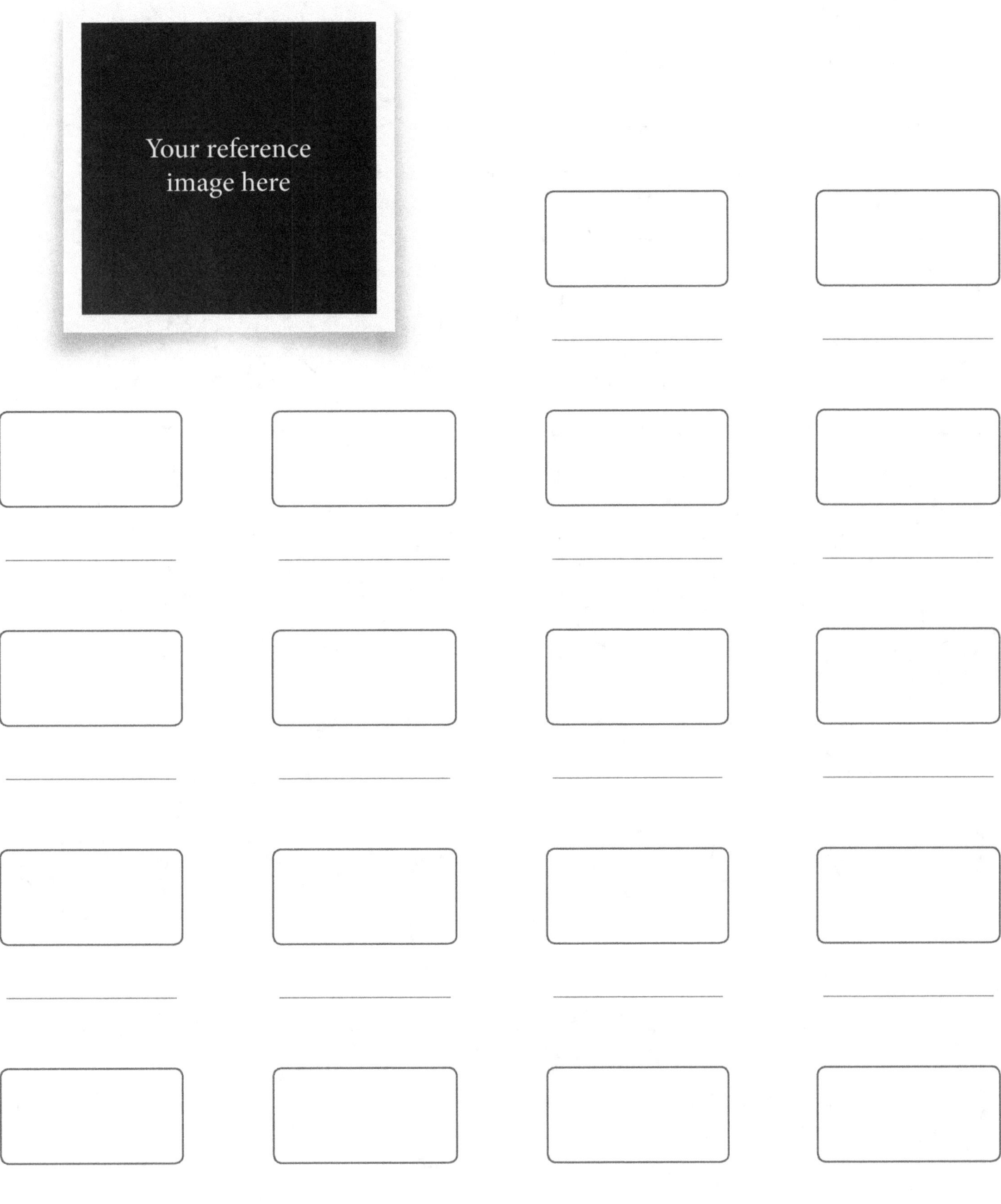

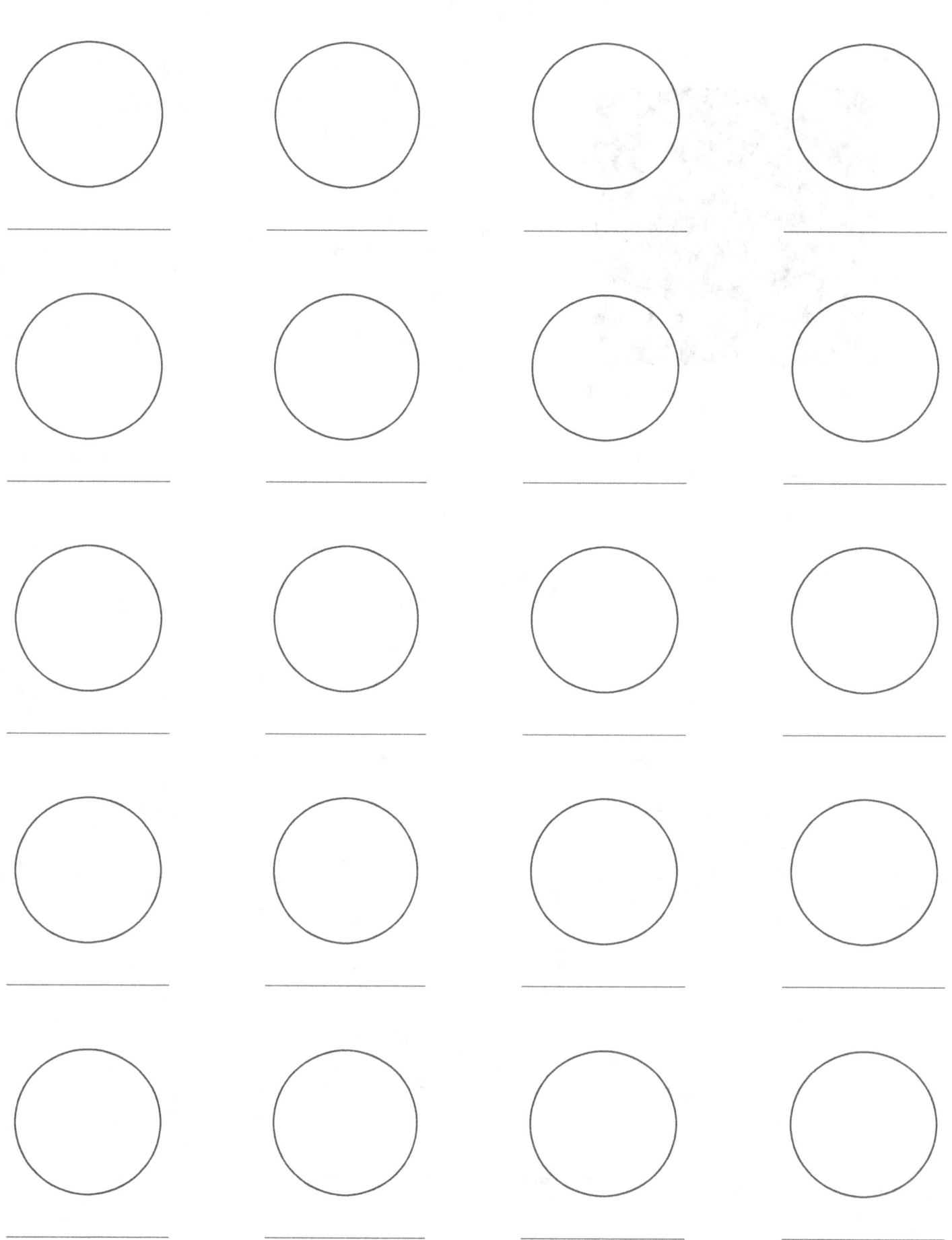

Your reference image here

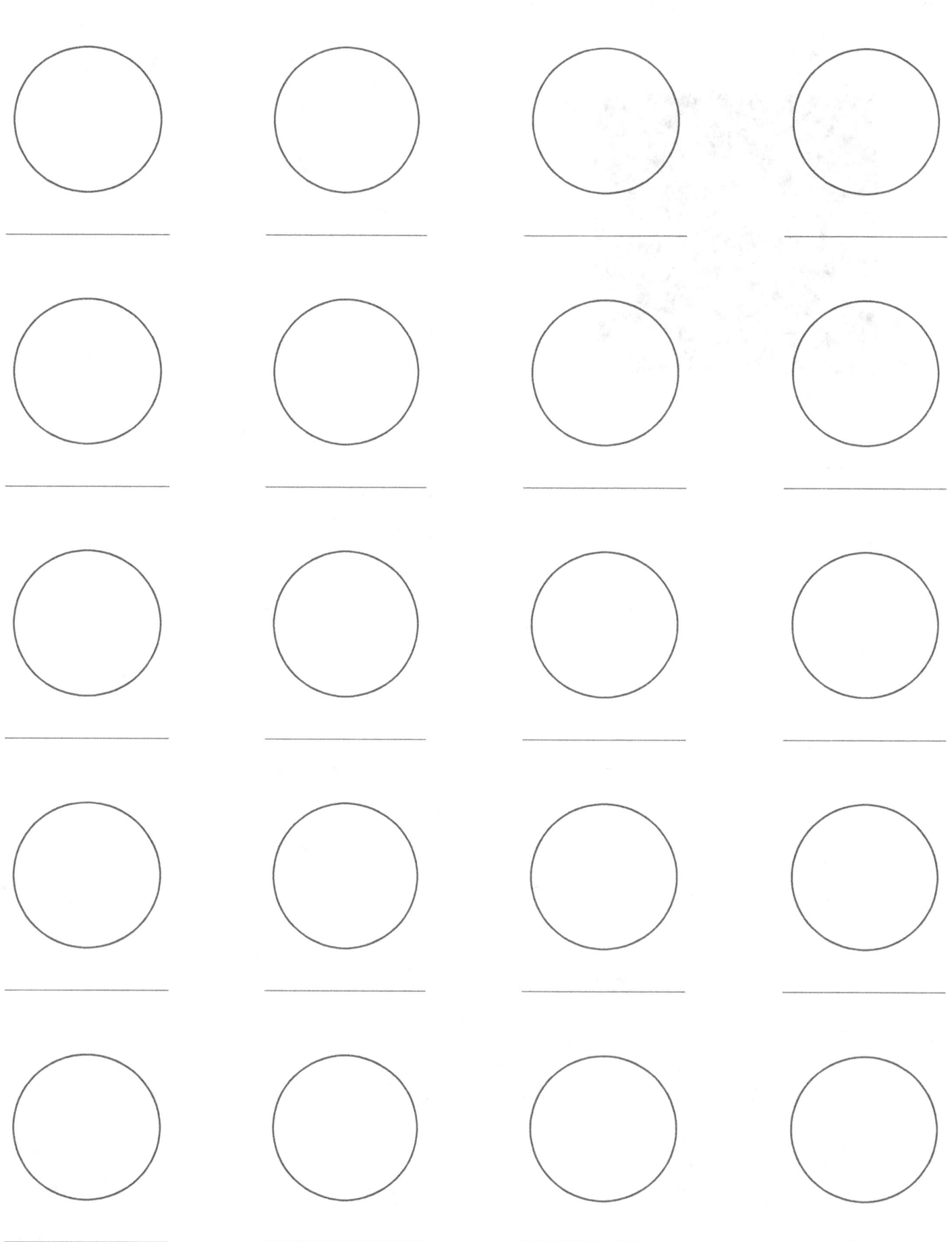

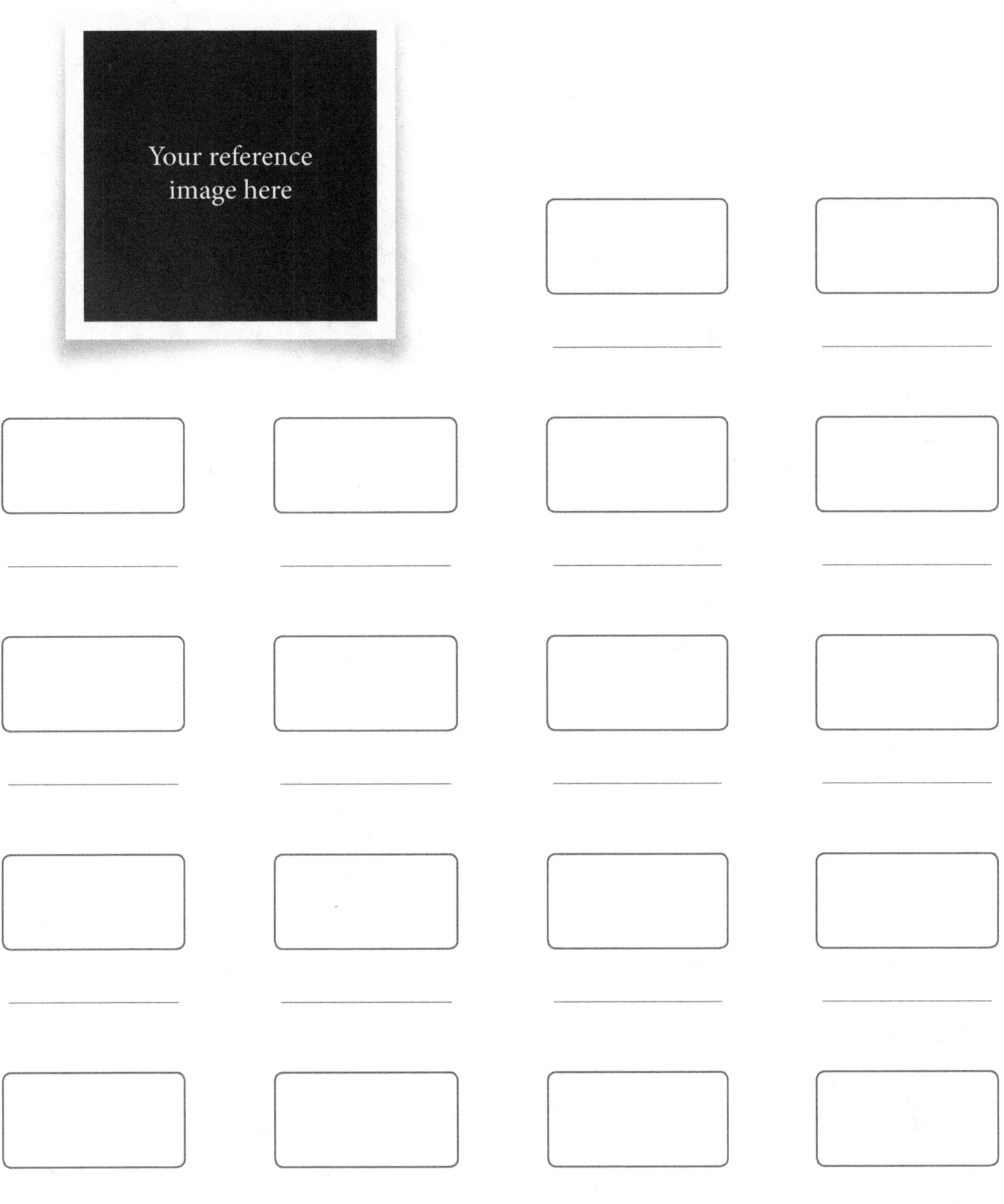

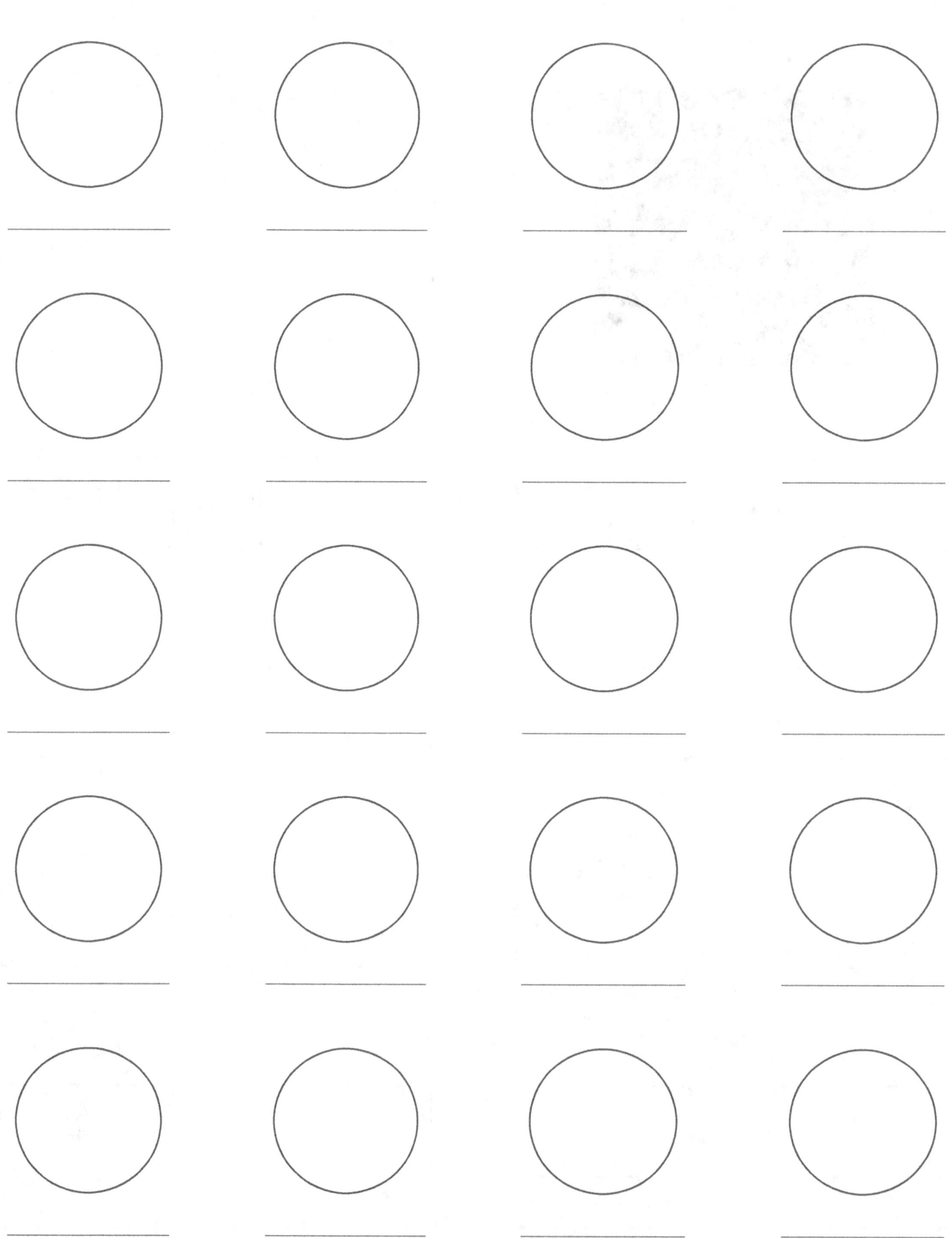

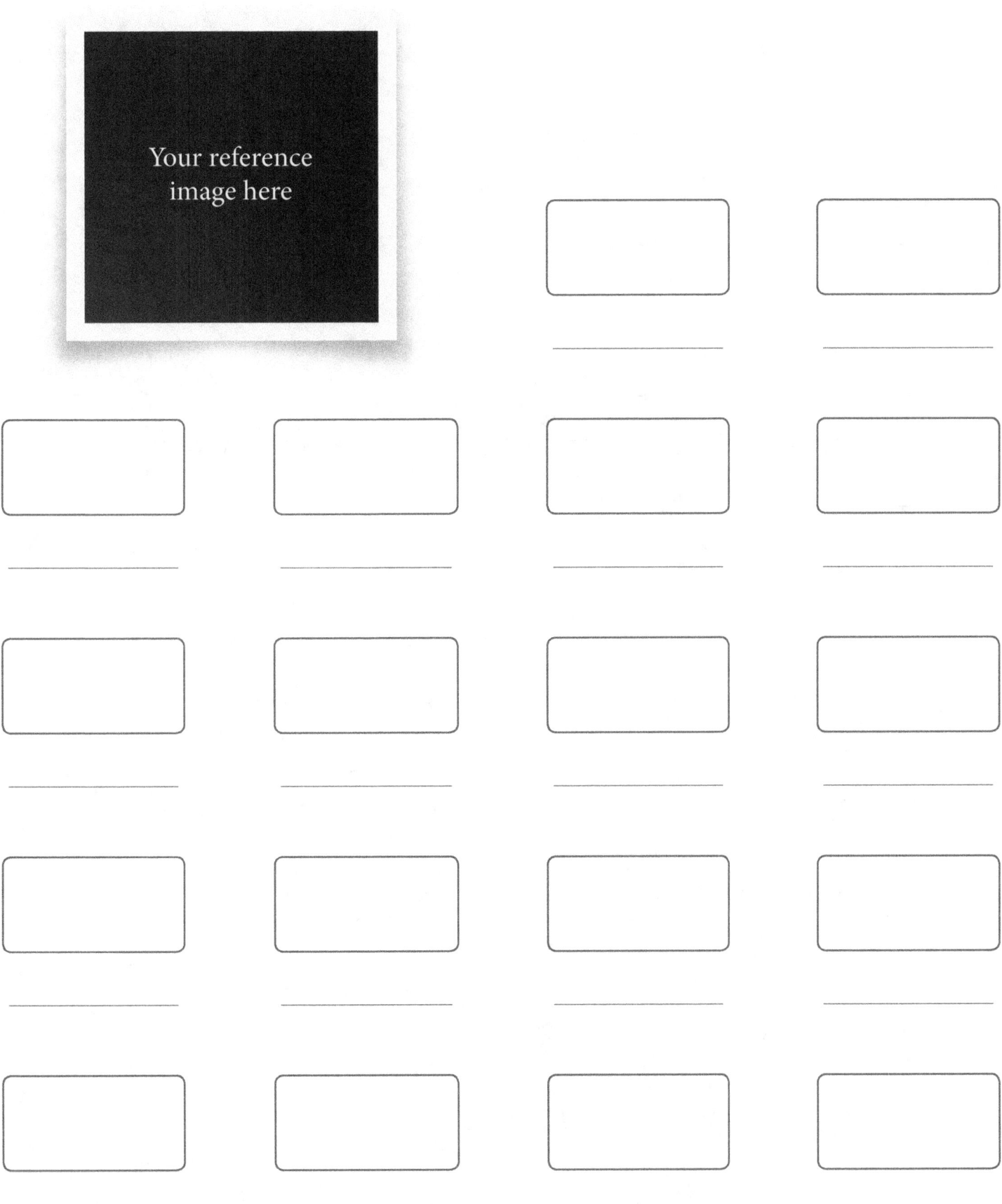

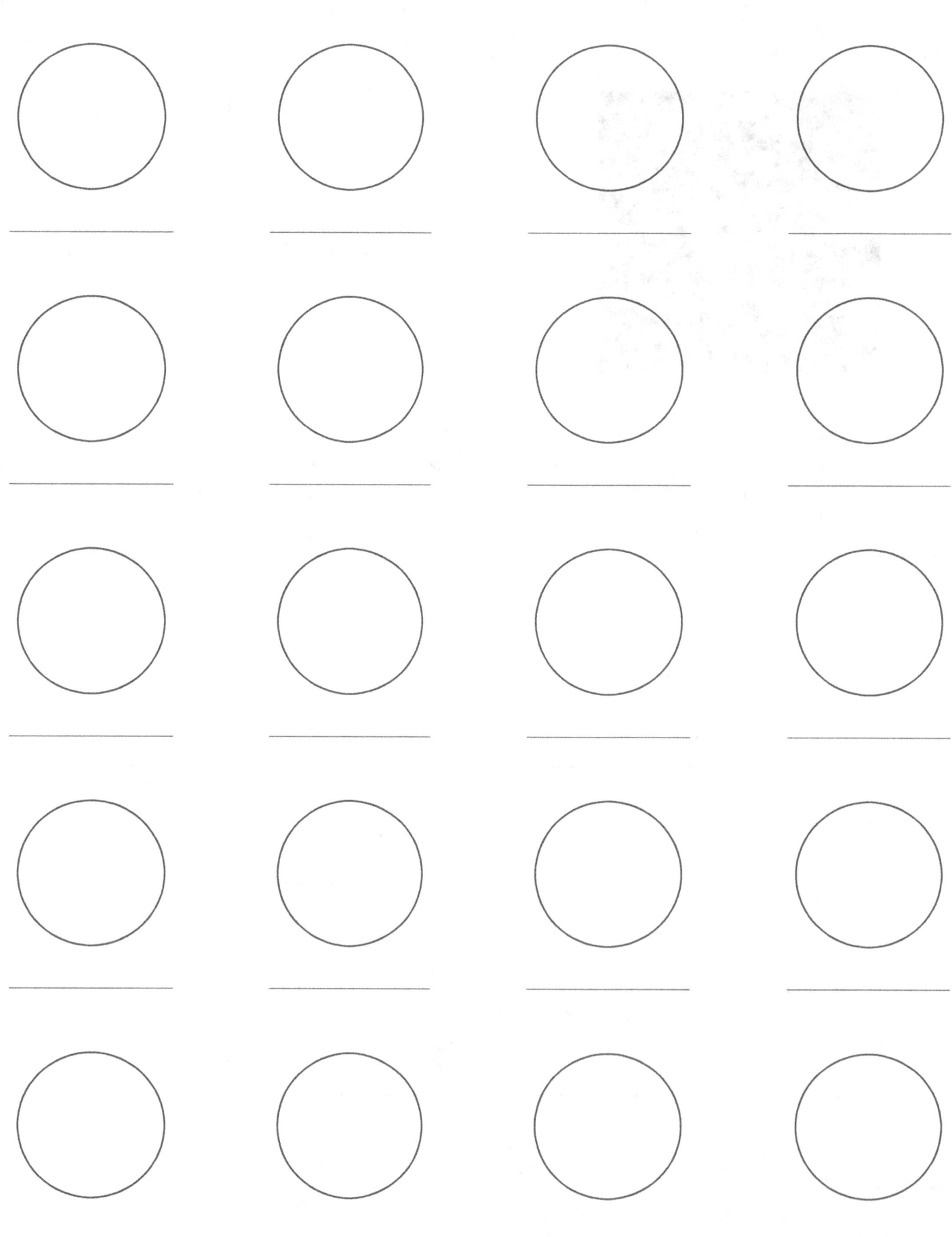

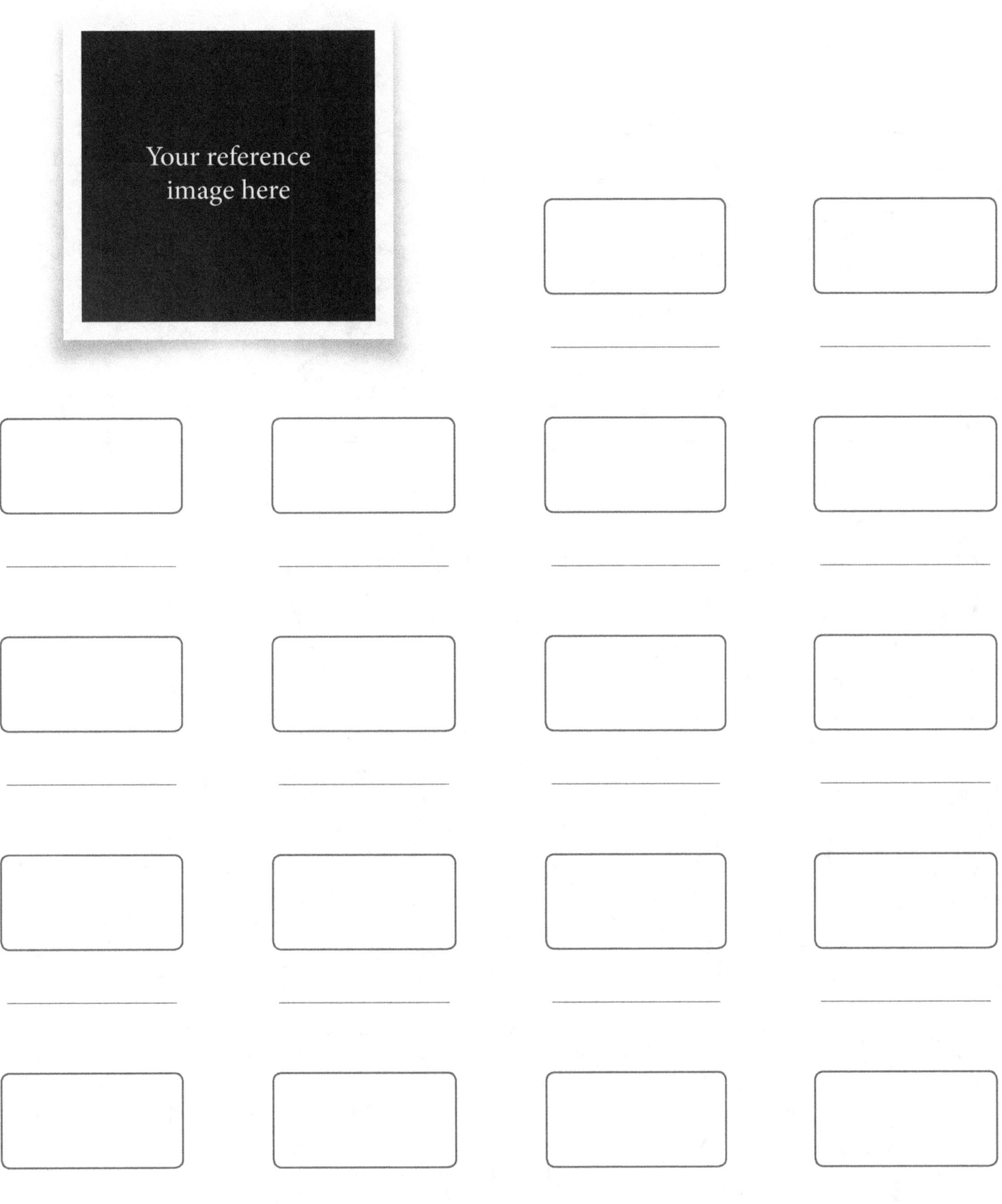

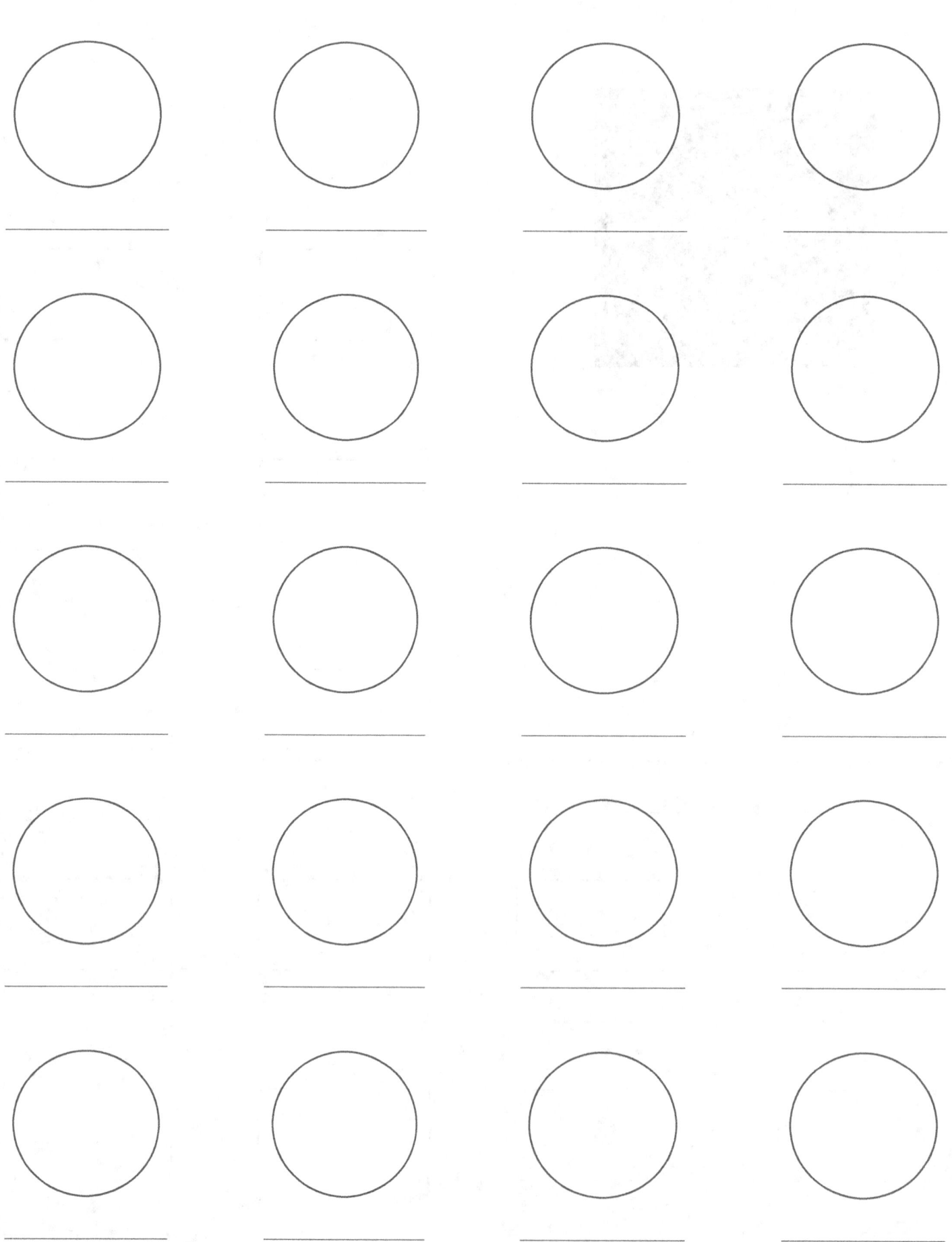

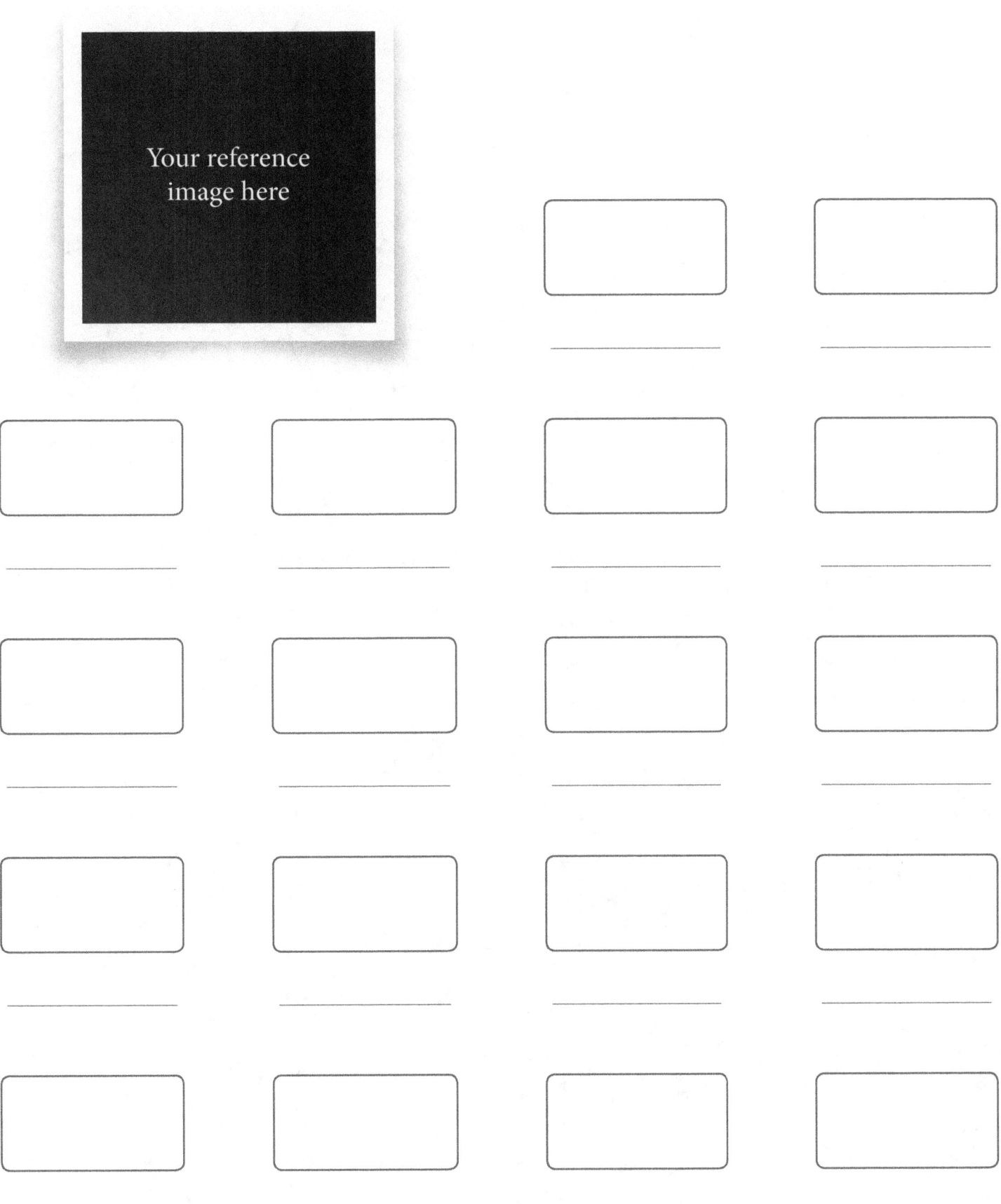

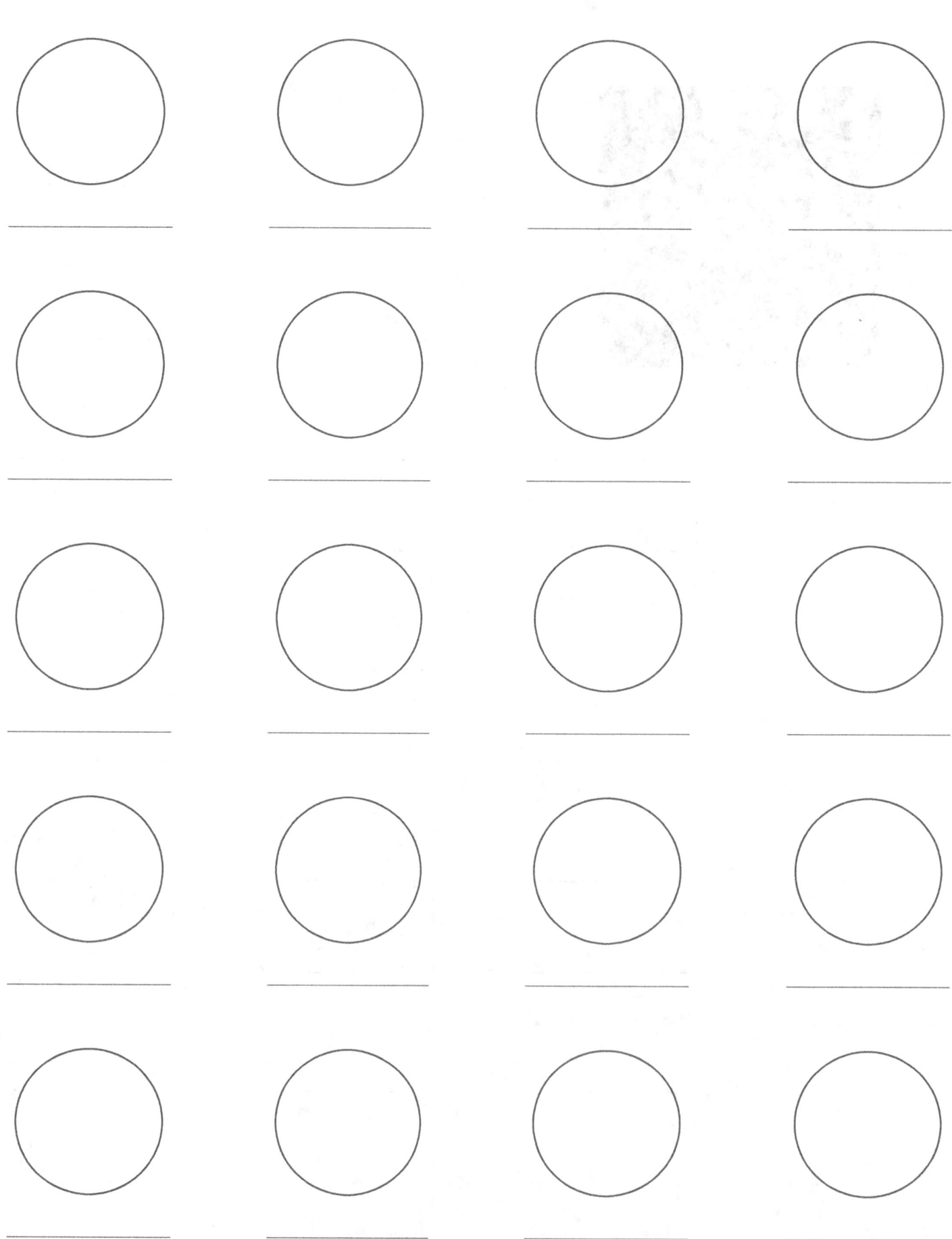

Your reference image here

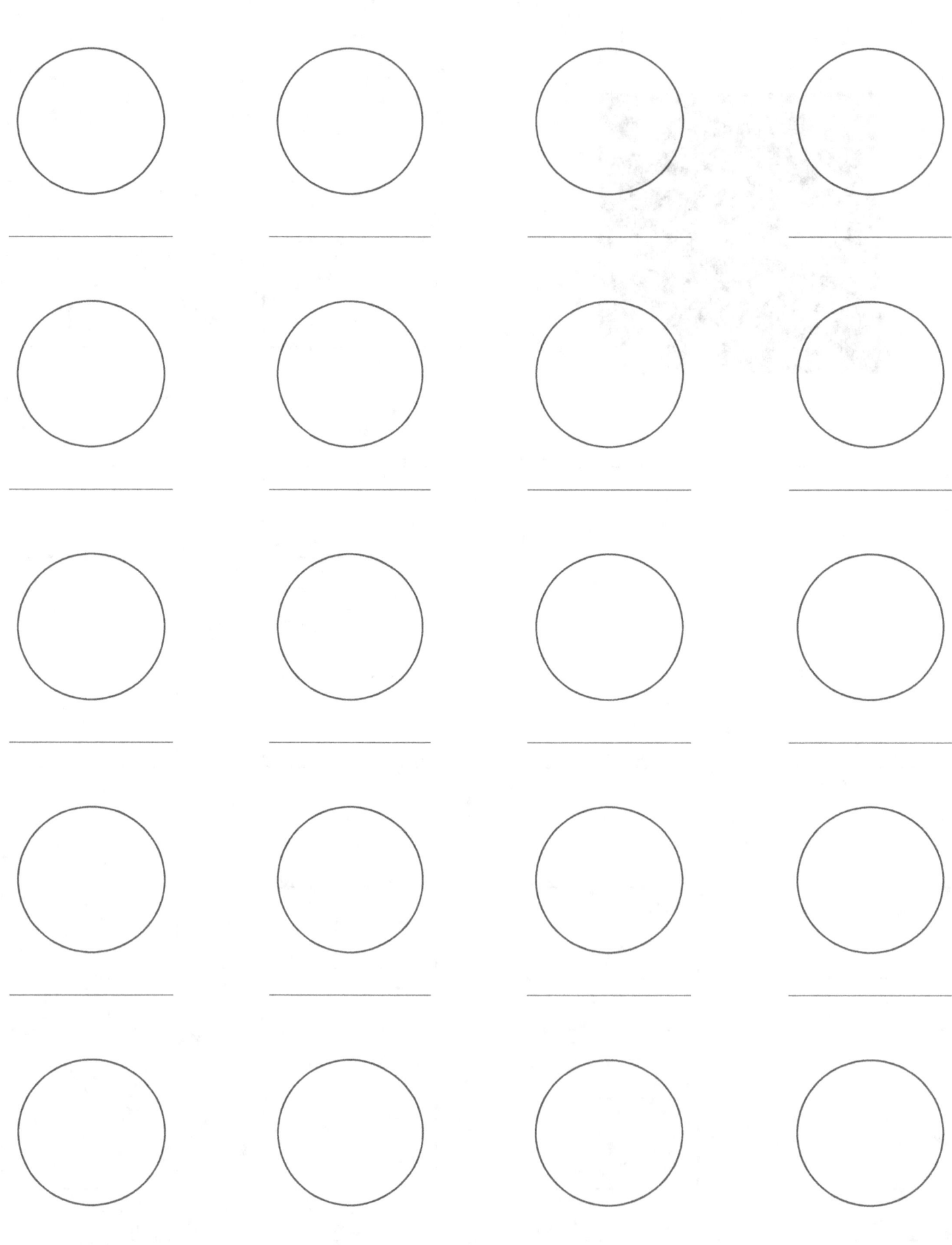

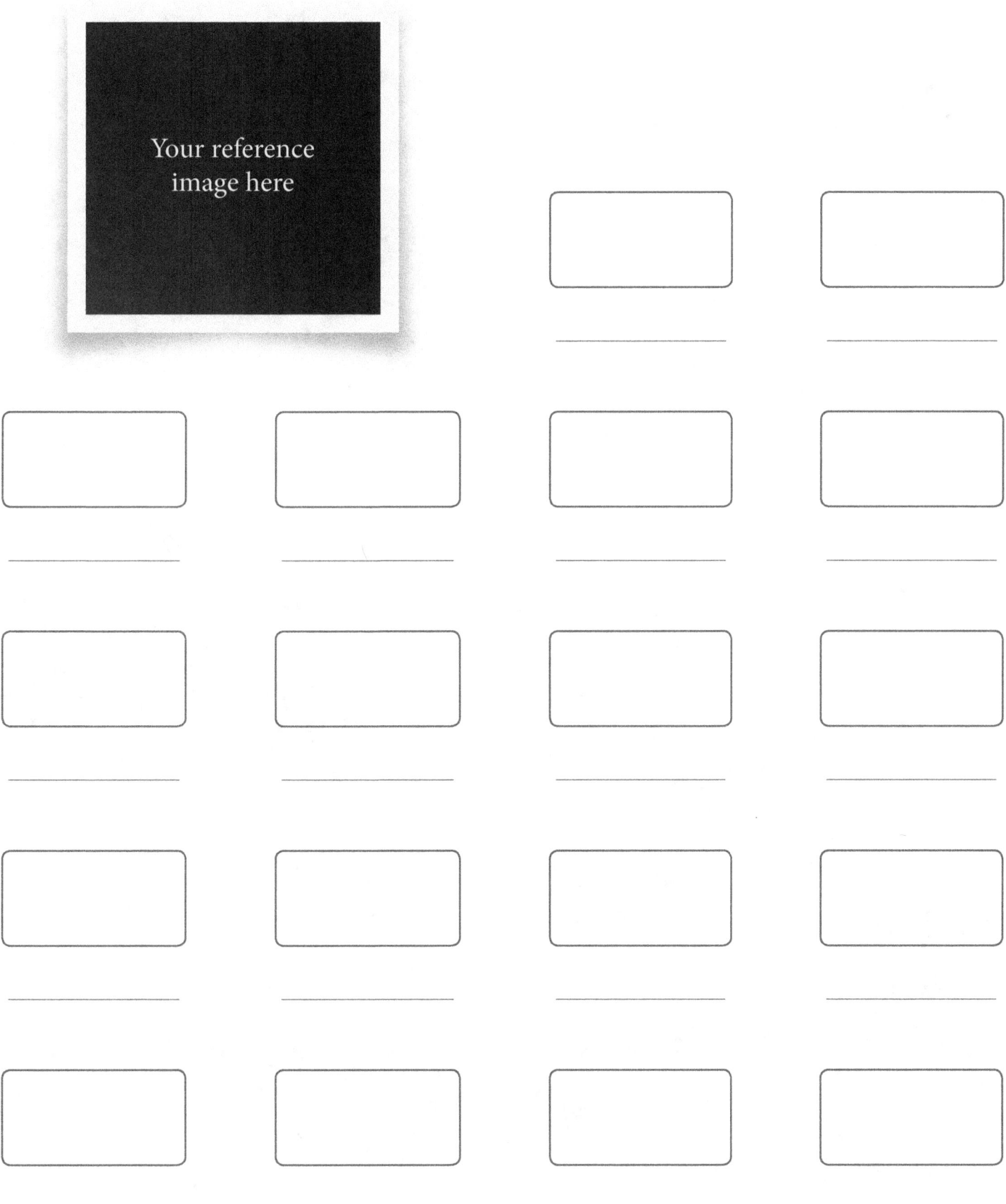

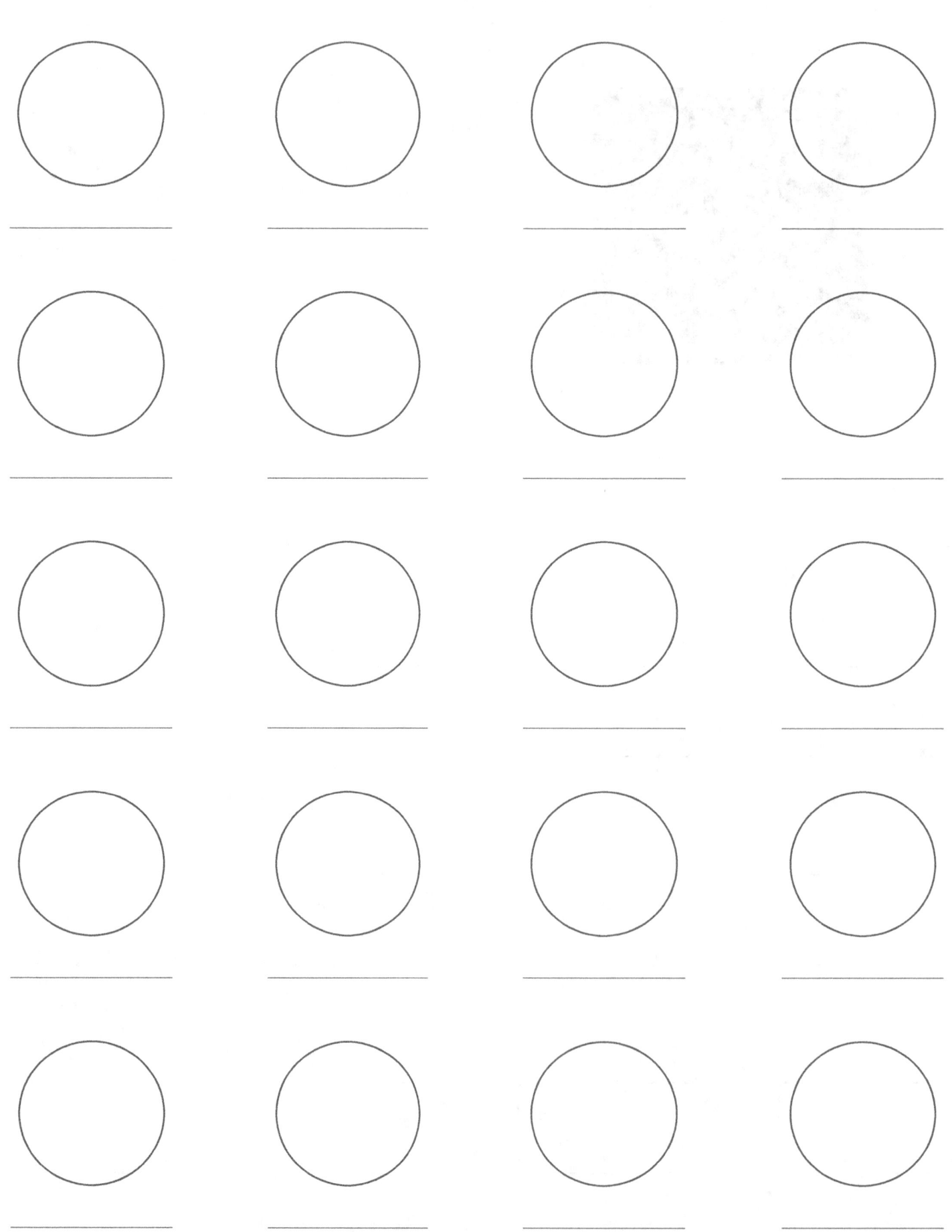

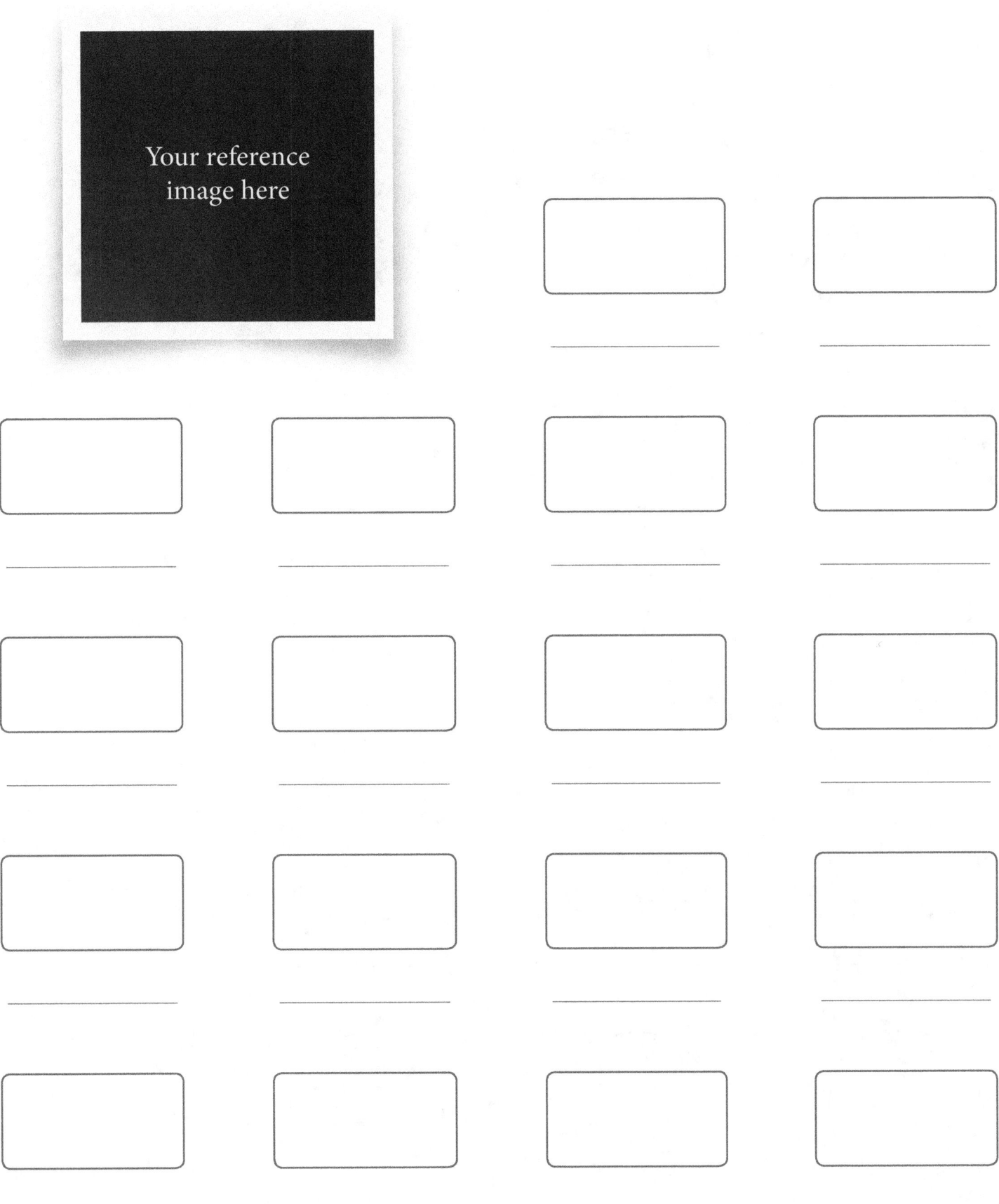

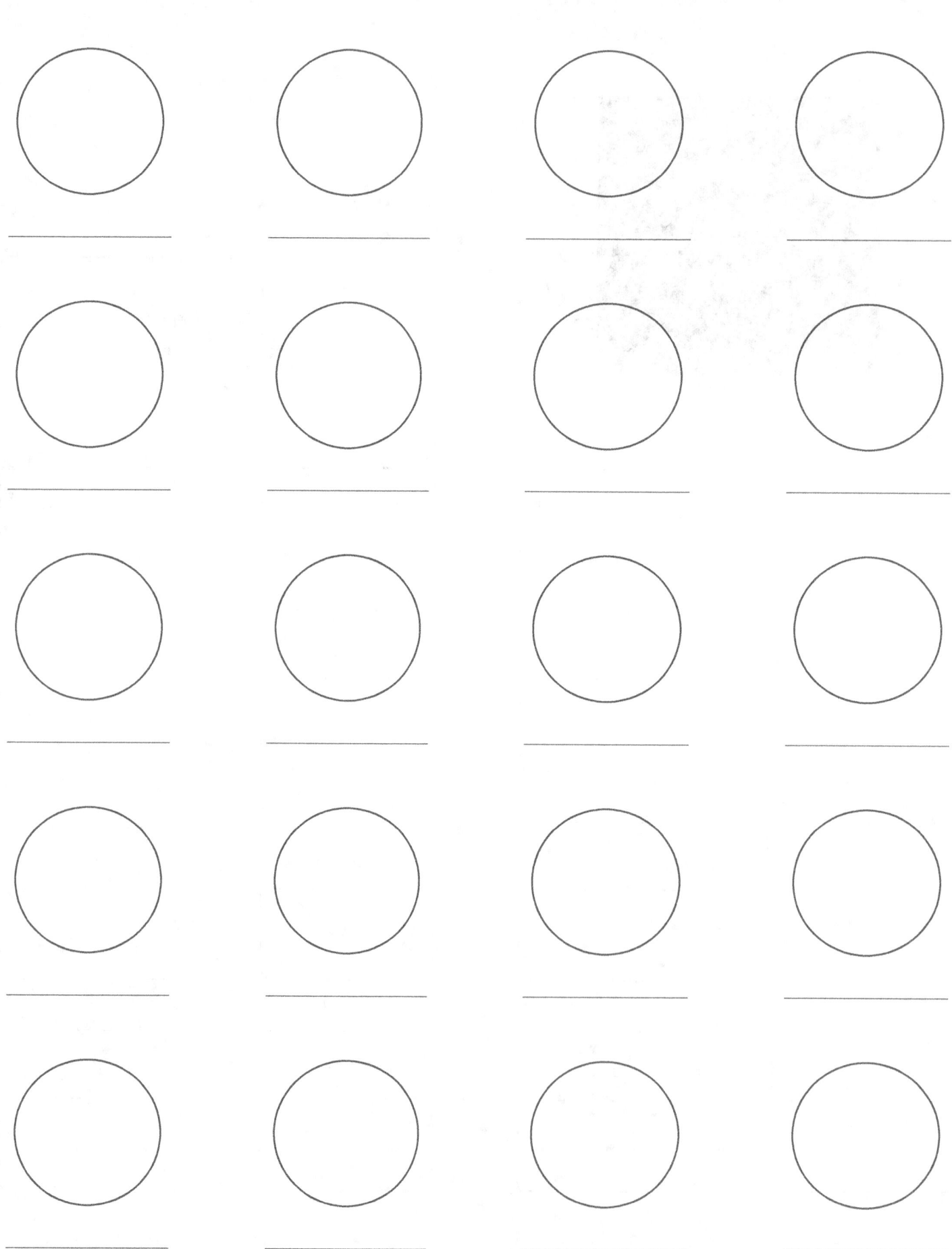

Your reference image here

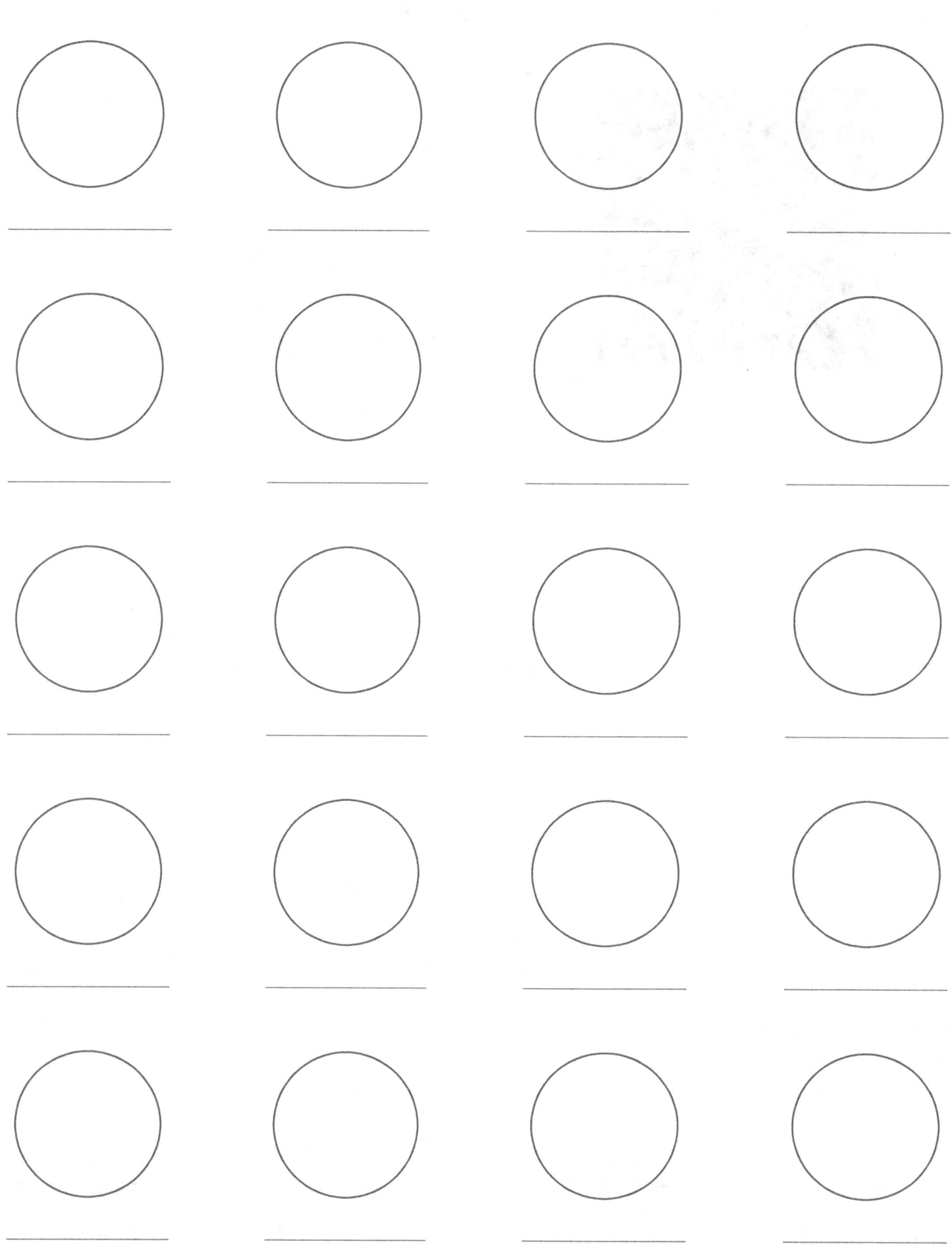

Your reference image here

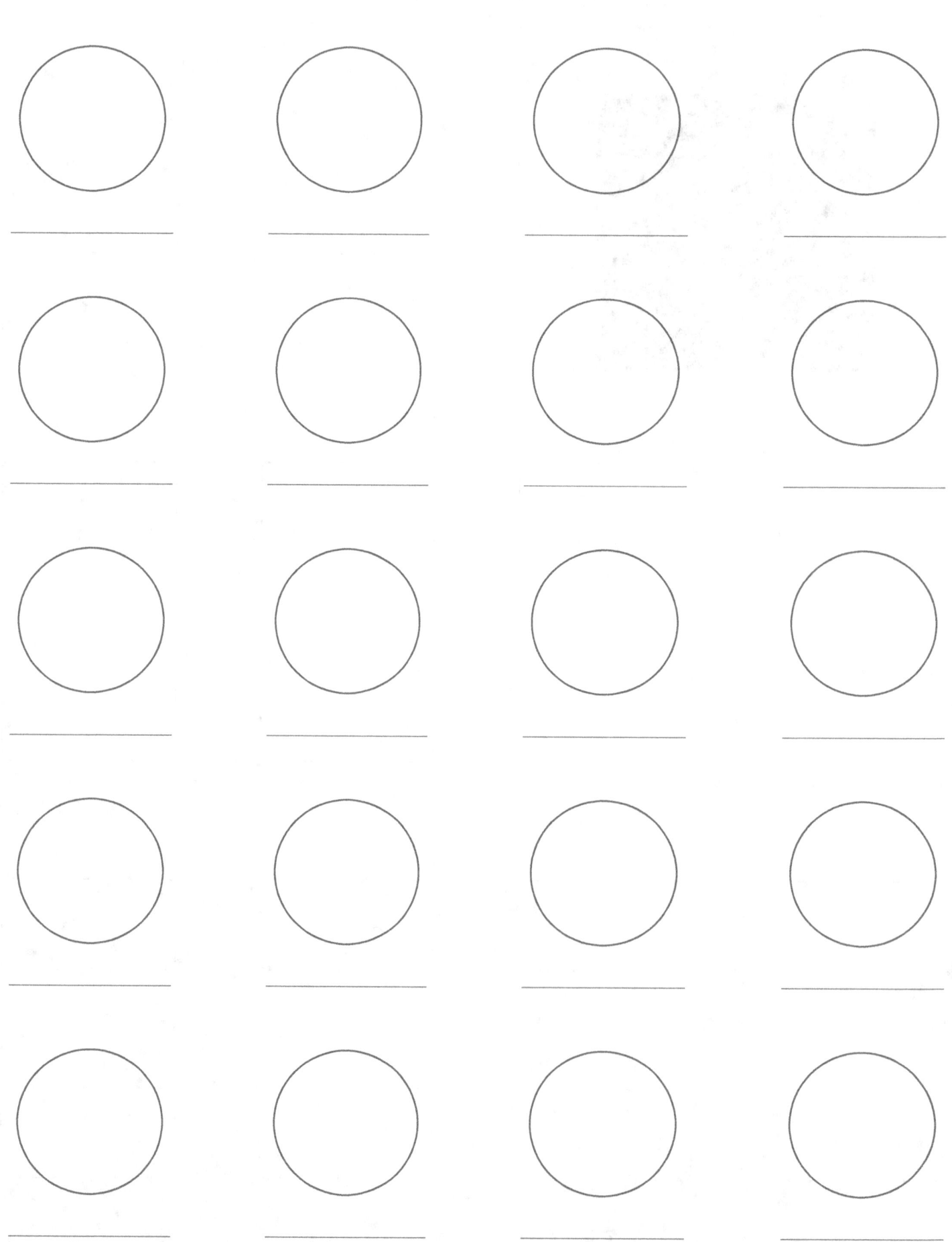